ACTA UNIVERSITATIS UPSALIEN
Studia Oeconomiae Negotiorum
41

D1543425

Michael Bromwich

ACCOUNTING FOR OVERHEADS

Critique and Reforms

UPPSALA 1997

ACTA UNIVERSITATIS UPSALIENSIS
Studia Oeconomiae Negotiorum
41

Michael Bromwich

⌈ACCOUNTING FOR OVERHEADS ⌋

Critique and Reforms

UPPSALA 1997

ABSTRACT

Bromwich, M. 1997. Accounting for Overheads. Critique and Reforms. Acta Universitatis Upsaliensis. *Studia Oeconomiae Negotiorum* 41. 102 pp. ISBN 91-554-3885-7.

This study urges that accounting reports within the firm should reflect the technologies underlying costs and uses this perspective to suggest new ways of accounting for overheads.

Michael Bromwich, Chartered Institute of Management Accountants' Professor of Accounting and Financial Management, Department of Accounting and Finance, London School of Economics and Political Science, Houghton Street, LONDON WC2A 2AE.

The Chartered Institute of
Management Accountants

Published with support from The Chartered Institute of Management Accountants (CIMA).

ISSN 0586-884X
ISBN 91-554-3885-7

Typesetting: Editorial Office, Uppsala University
Printed in Sweden by Gotab, Stockholm 1997
Distributor: Almqvist & Wiksell International, Stockholm, Sweden

Table of Contents

Acknowledgements   7

Preface   9

CHAPTER 1: Introduction   11
   The Structure of the Study   14

CHAPTER 2: Costs and Technology and Accounting for Variable
Resources   17
   Technology and Accounting   17
   Assumed Technology and the Character of Resources   19
      Operational Characteristics   20
      Supply Characteristics   20
      Managerial Characteristics   21
   Operational Characteristics   21
      Production Functions   22
      Output Independence   24
      Input Independence   25
      Independent Production   28
   Accounting for Variable Resources   30
      Operational Characteristics   32
      Input Separability   33
      Supply Characteristics   35
      Managerial Characteristics   36
      Limited Variable Inputs (Variant I in Table 2)   38
      Process Variable Resources (Variant II in Table 2)   42
   Activity Based Costing and Resource Use   42
   Relevancy of Resource Independence to
      Activity Based Costing   43
   Activity Costing and Product Volume   45

CHAPTER 3: Costs and Technology: Common and Joint Resources   49
   Common Resources   49
   Common and Joint Resources: Defined   49

Common Resources Variable with Outputs..................... 53
Fixed Resources in the Long and Short Runs 54
Common Resources and Non-Independence of Outputs........... 56
Common Resources: Outputs Ambiguous and
    Non-Measurable.. 58
Decision Driven Costs 61
Regulatory Resources..................................... 65
    Regulatory Requirements Which Impose Variable Costs 65
Joint Resources.. 66
Resources with Public Goods Characteristics 67
Costing Excludable Public Resources 70
The Use of Market Prices.................................. 71
Taxes on Public Resources................................. 74
    Lindahl Prices.. 74
    Ramsey Prices 75

CHAPTER 4: An Alternative Accounting Report and Conclusions 79
An Accounting Report Better Reflecting Technology.............. 79
Linking Inputs to Their Causes of Variation 80
Accounting Reports Reflecting the Technological Characteristics of
    Resources 88
Discussion of the Suggested Accounting Statement 92
Reforms and Conclusions.................................. 93
    Chapter 2 93
    Chapter 3 94
    Chapter 4 95

Bibliography.. 97

Acknowledgements

Many people have helped me in my wish to understand overheads. I am very grateful to many accountants in industry and commerce who have been willing to talk to me. Dr Miles Gietzmann and Dr Ian Tonks prepared working papers for me. I am also grateful to Bob Berry, John Christensen and Martin Loeb for reading an earlier manuscript. I am especially grateful to Anthony Atkinson, Bob Scapens and Charles Sutcliffe who commented in detail on a much fuller earlier draft.

I am also grateful to the CIMA reviewers who have to remain anonymous. I especially am grateful to Mai Lai (CIMA) who provided much research support and to my research assistant G Wang who prepared a number of working papers and provided much other research assistance. Any errors are my responsibility. I am also very grateful to Vera Bailey and Dorothy Richards who supervised the final draft of this study and typed much of it.

Finally, I wish to record my appreciation to CIMA for funding the project which gave rise to this study and waiting so patiently without complaint for this write up of some of the more theoretical findings of the project which was long in coming, and for financing the CIMA professorship at the London School of Economics and Political Science.

Preface

This study reports some of the findings of a project entitled *Accounting for Overheads especially in "High Tech" industries* funded by the Chartered Institute of Management Accountants. These findings formed the basis for my lectures at Uppsala in October 1993. I was very pleased to be invited to provide an accounting component to this series of important lectures reflecting the long and successful interest at Uppsala in accounting teaching and research.

I am very grateful to Ingemund Hägg and his colleagues who were very fine hosts and who provided much stimulating discussion which has helped me in writing up these lectures.

I am also very grateful for the patience and support they extended to me when delivery of the study was delayed due to an accident

CHAPTER 1

Introduction

Discussion of the problems of how to account for overheads in an economically meaningful way has a very long history. Generally researchers have severely criticised the practical approach of allocating overheads on what are seen as arbitrary bases. Such criticisms seem to have little effect on Anglo-Saxon practice where many surveys indicate that the great majority of firms allocate overheads using very simple allocation bases which are generally production volume based such as labour or machine hours.

The first aim of this study is to adopt an economic perspective to look analytically at how technology imposes certain characteristics on overhead costs and on cost behaviour and at some of the general technological characteristics of the underlying resources which help to determine the behaviour of different types of overhead costs. The aim here is to look at the structure imposed by technology on different types of resources which underlie overhead costs and help determine how and with what overhead costs vary. The aim is to look at the general rather than detailed characteristics of the technology which help determine the cost structure of the firm. Thus the emphasis will be on the general structures of production functions and how these structures affect costs. The second objective is to suggest accounting methods which reflect these factors whilst minimising any distortion in decision making caused by methods of dealing with overheads. The emphasis will generally be on decision making to keep the size of the monograph within reasonable bounds. Thus a major objective is to investigate options in reporting overheads which may be substituted for the seemingly dominant practice of allocating most, if not all, overheads. Thus little time will be spent on discussing the possible roles of cost allocations. In this study, overhead allocation refers to assigning overhead costs to cost objects within a firm within a period. Allocation over time will not be focused on in any detail.

Entertaining this economic perspective and the sophistication of some of the problems encountered mean that what may seem to some readers some fairly advanced economic concepts are utilised. However, no attempt is made to deal with these concepts in any rigorous way. The emphasis is on understanding the utility of these concepts in helping to understand and explain the behaviour of overhead costs. References to more rigorous treatments are given (see for example Banker and Hughes 1994, and Christensen and Demski 1995). However, this study shares a concern with a number of recent studies to treat cost analysis in a more rigorous manner than has perhaps been the case in the recent past.

Two earlier monographs, jointly authored with Al Bhimani and published by the Chartered Institute of Management Accountants, are complementary to this study and are deliberately more practitioner orientated. The first, *Management Accounting: Evolution not Revolution* (Bromwich and Bhimani, 1989) reviews current practices and evaluates the potentialities of new ideas in management accounting focusing especially on Activity Based Costing (ABC) and its variants, such as Activity Based Management (ABM) and Activity Based Budgeting (ABB). The second entitled *Management Accounting: Pathways to Progress*, (Bromwich and Bhimani, 1994) as its title indicates, evaluates a number of suggestions which may improve the effectiveness and efficiency of management accounting. It provides also a less detailed but perhaps more user friendly introduction to some of the ideas in this study. This study uses short extracts from these publications as it does extracts from my article entitled 'The Economic Foundations of Activity Based Costing (ABC)' published in K Dellman and K P Franz (eds.) *Neuere Entwicklungen im Kostenmanagement* (Verlag Paul Haupt Bern, 1995). I am grateful for permission to reproduce these materials.

In this study generally, a decision making rather than control perspective will be adopted. Allocations may well have roles to play in the control area. Adopting a decision making perspective raises the problem of the role of overheads in short term reports. The concern with routine management accounting reports also requires an explicit consideration of the decision making time span of these reports and raises the important problem of selecting between costs for the same items which appear when different decision making time spans are considered. Accounting reports tend to freeze the decision span upon which the reports are based. A later recommendation towards reconciling the different costs for different decision spans is that accountants might experiment with 'flexing' their figures, not only for volume but also for different decision time spans. This concern with short term reports also requires a consideration of how to report costs for existing overhead resources.

The starting point for the general analysis is the economic view that the two major factors influencing the costs structures of firms are technology and the prices of inputs (strictly, relative prices). When all inputs are variable; technology determines the physically efficient sets of resources that can be used for a given output. The relative prices of the factors in each efficient bundle of inputs then determine which is the cost minimising set of variable inputs. The cost function for a given product which plots costs against output thus depends on technology and prices and not just on changes in output. Less generally, in the presence of fixed factors, technology will determine the efficient bundles of resources for output conditional upon the levels of available fixed factors and

12

upon the production environment more generally. Changes in constraints may appear as the available technology alters as the time span of decisions are lengthened.

Accounting reports tend to assume that the technology to be used has been selected and that this selection of the method of production allows for the relative prices of factors. The only item normally allowed to vary in accounting reports is the volume of output. This is a different perspective to that of the economist who also asks how resource usage will alter with changes in the variables and parameters constituting technology and with alterations in prices. A similar view is taken by accountants in the German tradition when they ask how production may be best adapted for changes in output and other matters such as production mix. This concern with the various ways technology changes lies behind a later suggestion that accountants should consider flexing their reports for items other than just output.

Although accounting reports generally assume a given technology, this technology will be an important determinant of the cost function and of its constituents. It is the assumed technology that determines how usage of individual resources will be expected to change with alterations in other variables, usually outputs. Thus, it is generally technology that determines cost behaviour. Accountants in budgeting assume a specific pattern of behaviour for costs and are therefore implicitly assume a known technology for resources usage in their cost determination. Thus, treating items as variable costs (with no price changes) implies that their associated underlying resources vary in direct proportion to output.

Generally, at least in the accounting literature, implicit assumptions about technology remain hidden and are neither discussed nor considered. It is a fundamental premise of this study that accounting should reflect the technology of the resources being reported upon as otherwise accounting may provide distorted figures for decision making and control relative to a model that correctly reflects technology. It is the essence of Activity Based Costing and its variants, all of which will be referred to under the generic name of ABC in this study, to treat costs which were usually and generally dealt with as fixed costs instead as directly variable with some cost object. This is a clear statement that the traditionally assumed technology used with these costs was incorrect and the correct technology should be reflected in accounting. It is usually argued that such changes yield better figures for decision making.

It is argued in this study that there are many different types of resources with different underlying technologies which may require very different accounting treatments. It is difficult to believe that all those costs that are treated as overheads and which are allocated on the same basis share the same technology. This concern with technology in accounting is, perhaps, timely given the many pleas for accounting to reflect the new technical processes and methods being used by more and more firms.

Thus, a major objective of this study is to begin the process of seeking to

13

reflect the technology of resources in accounting reports. The focus is on the technological conditions which give resources the characteristics of overheads and therefore mean that their costs must be treated in different ways to those costs which can be traced to output volume or activity volume. However this requires that the technological characteristics underlying all generic types of costs be investigated so that those factors which are generally associated with overheads can be determined. The essence of the approach is therefore first to indicate what technological conditions are necessary and sufficient for costs to be traced to units of production (direct costs) or to the volume of a process or an activity (activity costs). The second stage is to analyse the costs of those resources which cannot be traced to units of either production or a specific activity. Possible accounting approaches for non-direct and non-activity costs are then considered. This approach will be seen to have much to say about overheads as generally the technologies of the overhead resources have not been investigated in any depth in accounting except by that school of accounting thought which urges the use of mathematical programming methods in dealing with, at least, some classes of overheads. Similarly, the analysis throws some light on the technological conditions that have to apply if the assumptions of ABC can legitimately be entertained.

The Structure of the Study

Chapter 2 seeks to examine various technical characteristics that can be used to describe different classes of resources which are then used in the following chapters. The general classification of characteristics of resources is based upon (i) the operational characteristics of resources, (ii) their supply attributes and (iii) their ease of management. It is shown that certain operational characteristics and supply attributes are necessary before resources, and therefore costs, can be traced to cost objects.

This chapter then uses these resource characteristics to determine the resource assumptions underlying a variety of familiar cost categories in accounting; those of resources variable with production volume and with process volume. The aim is to determine which of the resource characteristics are necessary for resources to behave as assumed by accountants for different classes of resources and their costs. Much of accounting entertains very specific but implicit assumptions about technology. The resource categories underlying certain types of costs chosen for study in a number of chapters are those inputs variable with output, those variable with activities or processes, common resources which may or may not be traceable to cost objects and which may be difficult to manage, and resources which display jointness either with other resources or between cost objects.

One important finding in Chapter 2 is that the conditions for resources and therefore costs to be traceable to units of output are very restrictive including that the use of the resource is independent of the level of use of other inputs and of the volume of production of other products. Moreover, these conditions seem to be the same as those which must apply to activity or process variable resources and costs. This suggests that few of the new types of costs generated by the changing manufacturing environment are likely to be able to be treated as variable with product or activity outputs, thus adding to the accountant's existing problems. In contrast, there seems no reason to treat those common resources which can be traced to cost objects as overheads requiring allocation. They should therefore be treated as costs direct with production or activity volumes.

Three new problems with ABC are identified in this chapter. The first is that it can be demonstrated that the cost of an activity output represents an incremental cost of some cost object at what may be a high level of the cost object hierarchy. Practice often attempts to link such costs to the costs objects for which the activity is provided (say, product units), below the level of the cost object at which the activity cost becomes incremental. This process represents an allocation though, perhaps, one with only relatively minor effects. The second problem is that contrary to what ABC proponents claim, it is not obvious that volume related and activity related functions can be treated as if they were independent of each other. Substantial changes in production volume are likely to require associated alterations in related activity outputs and, indeed, in the way such activities are organised. For example, a large change in volume is likely to have an impact on supply and logistic activities and on planning activities. Similarly, changes in the organisation of activities may affect feasible production volume.

The third problem is that although output variable costs can be directly related to the revenue generated by the products which incur these costs, activity costs can only be directly linked to the activity output with which they are associated and are not directly related to revenues generated by the firm. Many ABC proponents have sought to overcome this problem by either allocating activity costs to the products to which they contribute, with all the familiar problems, or by seeking to determine whether or not activities add value but this requires that organisational cash flows can be attributed to activities. The temptation is to seek to do this by again allocating activities to products.

Chapter 3 considers common resources which both can and cannot be treated as traceable to outputs or processes. It also considers joint resources which are shown to have resource characteristics which are difficult to account for in an economically meaningful way. The conventional methods of allocating overheads to products seem not consistent with these characteristics as these methods come down to treating these resources as if they were variable with output volume. A major conclusion of this part of the project is that resources exhibiting jointness can be treated in a number of ways.

Another theme taken up in Chapter 3 is that of 'difficult to manage' resources which have ambiguous outputs which are difficult to link to organisational goals. The technology of these resources may be difficult to understand and may produce ill-defined outputs. The costs of such resources tend to be treated as overheads and a technological and cost structure is imposed upon them in allocating them to cost objects. A number of other ways of dealing with these resources are considered in this study.

The final chapter seeks to design an accounting report which incorporates much of the foregoing analysis. This requires first that various types of resources discussed above are linked up to their causes of variations (their cost drivers in modern parlance). This exercise shows that different types of resources are substantially affected by different cost drivers. Resources variable with output and activities are mainly affected directly by cost drivers including product volume, activity or process intensity and the composition of the model or product programme. Common resources which cannot be traced to product or process outputs and joint resources are suggested to be mainly affected by decisions to supply either manufacturing capacity or the capacity to provide other services. This linking of resources to their causes of variation allows technology to be reflected in accounting and suggests that different types of resources should be accounted for in different ways.

An aim of the suggested accounting statement is to collect together costs which share a common technology and to reflect this technology in the accounting methods being used for these resources. The second aim is to reduce the number of resources and related costs which are treated as overheads and allocated as in conventional accounting. The suggested accounting report regards as traceable only those costs that can be treated as incurred solely for the cost object in mind, and collects together those costs traceable to the same cost object. Costs variable with capacity decisions are reported separately from other costs because the accounting for these may be very different from that used for other cost categories.

The entertained cost categories are used to provide a hierarchy of contributions which indicate whether each cost category is covered by revenue generated by its associated cost object. Each of these contributions should relate to a relatively separable part of the firm and ideally should relate to similarly separable managerial responsibilities.

CHAPTER 2

Costs and Technology and Accounting for Variable Resources

The first part of this chapter looks at the impact of the firm's technology on its cost structure and therefore on the accounting that might be used to reflect technology. As was indicated in the introduction, the focus of this report is upon routine periodic management accounting reports as these represent the major and continual outputs of management accounting departments and decision making based thereon. Overhead allocations often play a large role in these reports. This part of the chapter presents a number of characteristics of resources and of technology which need to be considered if accounting is to be consistent with enterprise technology. It does this by looking at the basic characteristics of the enterprise's technology and by generating hypotheses which allow the categorisation of different types of costs based on some general technological characteristics. Later parts of this chapter and Chapter 3 use this classification of technology and resources to examine the sets of assumptions describing resource and technological characteristics which are needed to define certain familiar cost categories in accounting.

To ease the presentation, the terms resources, factors and inputs will be used synonymously. Used without qualification the term variable should be understood to mean variable with output. Similarly, the term volume used without qualification and the term product volume will refer to the output of either final or intermediate goods.

Technology and Accounting

Although this part of the study is addressed primarily to resources and not cost, some implications for costs of studying resources will be presented. Technology is a major determinant of the firm's cost structure. The relationship between technology and cost is best illustrated by the fact that correctly defined cost functions of the firm where factor prices are allowed to vary can be shown to contain all the information that would be obtained by studying directly the firm's technology. The cost function referred to here is more general than that which is normally used in accounting which assumes that factor prices are

17

fixed. The usual cost function produces cost curves which are a function of only product volume (see Chambers, 1988, pp. 82–86 and Krouse, 1990, pp. 35–36). More generally, the choice of the least cost method of production for a given output can be seen as proceeding in two steps. First, all the efficient bundles of variable inputs that may be used for a given output are ascertained and then the least cost combination of factors for the given output is chosen as the method of production for the output. Thus, the demands for each factor depend on factor prices and desired outputs and are conditional on the optimal levels of the other factors used in production. The economist's cost function relating outputs to input costs thus portrays the costs of least cost, and technological efficient bundles of inputs for each output for each set of factor prices. In economics, the firm's technology is, thus, accorded a crucial role in determining the cost function. This is in contrast to accounting where technology seems to be relegated to being a background factor. Intuitively, this technology can be discovered by looking at cost functions because the optimal set of variable inputs for each set of input prices will represent that bundle of inputs from the firm's technology which represents the cost minimising way of producing a specific output given the set of factor prices. Thus, each input bundle in the cost function represents one efficient way of using the firm's technology. Determining the efficient set of inputs from the firm's technology in this way for each possible set of input prices yields all the efficient bundles of resources contained in the firm's technology. This indicates that the other determinant of cost structure in addition to technology is relative factor prices.

This process, thus, allows the discovery of all efficient bundles of resources utilising only information contained in the cost function. Economists use this relationship to learn about technology as cost functions are believed to be easier to observe than enterprise technologies. Here the process is reversed by studying technology in order to learn about the specification of enterprise cost functions so that they may correctly reflect enterprise technology. This approach is also adopted because of the many criticisms that traditional cost functions no longer reflect modern technology. Indicating the technological assumptions underlying the conventional cost function and comparing these with those of current technology helps to assess this criticism. Determining the cost functions implied by modern technologies helps in evaluating how far the suggested reforms of accounting to reflect for modern technology do encompass the characteristics of this technology and validly incorporate it into revised cost functions. As costs and profits reflect not only technology but also prices, a later part of this chapter will consider if accounting reflects not only sensible assumptions about technology but also about factor prices.

The ultimate aim of this part of the chapter is to present and analyse the technological characteristics of the various inputs that may be used by the firm. The technological characteristics of different classes of inputs are argued to constrain the accounting treatment that can be applied to the costs of these inputs if it is wished costs to reflect that technology.

This understanding of the character of resources is used later to suggest

18

reforms to accounting which reflect the enterprise's technology. That such reforms emerge represents no great surprise as current technology is often very different to the implied technology that underlies conventional management accounting techniques. Modern technology incorporates many new material and component flow planning models and resource planning methods (for example, MRP II), computer aided design and manufacture (CAD/CAM) and computerised planning and control methods and new methods of manufacture, such as advanced management technology (ATM) including computerised numerically controlled machines (CNC), robotics and production cells, flexible manufacturing systems (FMS) and ultimately computer integrated manufacture (CIM). Similar, and perhaps more radical, changes are occurring in the service industries and indeed in the service departments and sectors of manufacturing industry (see, for example, Child and Loveridge, 1990). All these changes have simultaneously increased the number and quality of information flows through the organisation.

Recently, many commentators have sought to explore the implications of these changes for accounting. They are generally agreed that the modern manufacturing environment reduces very substantially those enterprise costs which are variable with product volume in a specific time period and increases very substantially other costs, especially those which have been treated as fixed costs in traditional accounting. Many of these commentators have sought to suggest accounting reforms. Many of these are proving of substantial utility in practice but they may not have fully tackled needed changes in accounting for overheads. This and the next chapter, especially Chapter 3, suggest that this is because this cost category encompasses a wide variety of resources with rather different characteristics which have not been fully reflected in extant accounting. Reforms will be suggested which capture the richness of the component parts of overheads.

The next part of the chapter commences the substantive analysis of accounting and technology by presenting a number of characteristics which will be used to classify resources into resource types in this and the next chapter. The factors with which the use of these resources (and therefore their costs) may be variable will also be considered in these chapters. In both cases, accounting reforms suggested by these classifications will be considered. Combining these two classifications generates further suggestions for accounting reform in Chapter 4.

Assumed Technology and the Character of Resources

This part of the chapter considers some possible criteria which can be used to classify the character of resources. No pretence is made that the list of characteristics considered below is either comprehensive and exhaustive or represents anything other than a possibly useful classification scheme generally utilising concepts which have been found useful in economic theory and in empirical work in applied economics. Three general classifications will be used: (i) the operational characteristics of resources (ii) their supply attributes and (iii) their managerial characteristics. The first two sets of attributes build on a large literature in economic theory (see Ferguson 1979 and Chambers 1988).

Operational Characteristics

Operational characteristics include the relationship of resources to final goods outputs and to process outputs, to other inputs, the characteristics of the production of resources and whether resource use has any effects on the organisation's other activities.

Certain attributes of the operational characteristics of resources help to determine when the use of inputs is validly traceable to final goods or process outputs. They thus help determine the form of accounting that can be legitimately be applied to different types of resources in so far that it is wished that the assumptions of the accounting methods employed capture the characteristics of the resources. The operational characteristics which apply to specific resources depend on the time period considered in decision making. As the time period is lengthened, more uses of resources cease to be fixed with product or process output and became variable with output. Thus, many of the characteristics applying to an input are sensitive to the time period being considered.

Supply Characteristics

The second set of characteristics, the supply characteristics of resources, refer to attributes, such as, whether resources are traded in well organised markets and whether their supply to the enterprise is unconstrained. The accounting methods used with inputs should reflect these characteristics if accounting is intended to aid decision making and it is wished that decision making models are consistent with those advocated in economics. This category makes it clear that classifications of this type again depend on the time period being considered. Again, supply conditions for inputs will be conditional upon the length of the time period considered. Generally, the time period entertained here will be assumed to be sufficiently short so that not all resources are adjustable in the period as this seems to be the time period generally addressed by accounting.

The sensitivity of both operational and supply of characteristics to the time periods considered in decision making reinforces one important reform to accounting suggested above. It will be indicated later that a better understanding of the flexibility of resources and costs over time by management could be given by incorporating the effects of time into accounting reports. Given the

20

possible lack of connection between strategic planning and capital budgeting and the management accounting reporting system, in practice, such effects, if they are explored at all, in accounting practice are considered in *ad hoc* exercises and in any budgeting exercises which run beyond the conventional yearly time span.

Managerial Characteristics

This final general category refers to how easy the resources in mind are to manage and really restates the operational characteristics discussed above in a more managerial manner. Difficulty in management is suggested to depend on whether the outputs from resources are ambiguous or difficult to quantify, clearly related to firm objectives or difficult to trace to such objectives, and non-measurable or fuzzy, and therefore not easily measurable, whether the process in which inputs are used is repetitive or one-off and whether the technology involved is understood or not and therefore whether the effects of any managerial intervention in the process is understood. Again, the type of accounting that can be used with inputs will depend on these characteristics. Accounting at the present time has major difficulty with one-off processes without clear measurable outputs where the technology involved is not clearly understood. These characteristics apply to many centrally provided services.

Operational characteristics which reflect technology are now considered in a little more detail prior to using these characteristics to generate a number of tables where a number of types of resources are described in terms of these characteristics. The aim with these tables is to see under what conditions inputs can be traced to specific cost objects.

Operational Characteristics

Generally, in economics, variable inputs in any time period are assumed to be exclusively variable with the rate of output in that period, though this is not required in economic analysis, see, for example, Alchian, 1959, who argues that total planned volume of output and the scheduling of production also help explain production operations and Lewis, 1949, who indicates that public utility engineers at that time customarily divided costs into those which vary with volume, demand related standing costs (peak costs), customer costs and residual costs (1949, p. 14, footnote 1) and assigned each type of cost on a different basis. Nor are other factors impinging on the use of resources in a period unconsidered. For example, the amount of resources required per unit of output to achieve a certain level of quality per unit of output could form part of variable cost, though, ideally in decision making, such costs should represent long run variable costs (see Shaked and Sutton, 1986).

The economic emphasis placed on output intensity in a period may flow

21

from the view that most decisions, such as the amount of advertising or of resources devoted to selling are made at the beginning of the period and given these decisions only output or pricing decisions can be made during the period. Classical management accounting also considers variable resources to be altered only with the rate of output in the period but tends to use the associated costs for many other decisions, even though these variable costs are conditioned by the decisions about other items made at the beginning of the period. Using such costs in decision making without adjustment for the likely levels of other variables which impinge on these costs is likely to distort the input and cost effects of any decisions.

This possibility introduces a major theme of this study which is that any use of accounting numbers imports the conditions under which these costs were generated into any other utilisation of these numbers. Much of this and the next chapter are devoted to presenting some of these conditions and to indicating that these are much more complex than is, perhaps, usually expected. The existence of this complexity suggests that routinely produced accounting figures should not be used in a context where the environment that conditioned the original figures does not apply.

Production Functions

In order to discuss operational characteristics, it is necessary to have a little understanding of what are called production functions in economics. These are therefore briefly described below.

Generally, in economics, technology is captured by the concept of a production function which assumes that the time period considered is such that all inputs may be taken as variable. This function indicates the maximum volume of the output that can be generated from any arbitrary bundle of inputs. It can be written

$$y = f(x_1, x_2, ..., x_n)$$

Where y is the product output and may represent one product or a set of products. x_i stands for the various variable inputs from which output can be manufactured. It is assumed that both inputs and outputs are non-negative and that a unique and definite output can be associated with any specific combinations of inputs. (See Chambers, 1988, pp. 7–8 and Ferguson, 1979, pp. 7–8.) More generally, the relationship between inputs and output will depend on the level of the non-variable inputs assumed. Thus the maximum level of output that can be obtained from a specific bundle of labour and materials will be dependent on the amounts of fixed equipment, plant and production capacity available, the configuration of these fixed inputs and the production infrastructure generally. The optimal output from a given combination of factors may also depend upon decisions contained in the production plan, and more generally, on the production environment.

22

A more general representation of the production function including these factors and other elements of the production environment can be written as

$$y = F(x_1, x_2, \dots, x_n; \bar{z}_i, \dots, \bar{z}_m; E_i, \dots, E_k)$$

Here z_i, represents fixed factors, where the bar over the z indicates their fixity and the E_i represent environmental factors.

Production functions assume that any bundle of inputs is used in the most efficient way to produce output. They thus utilise different assumptions to those made in budgeting where generally only a feasible degree of efficiency is assumed. Production functions capture technology in the sense that they express the physical relations between inputs and outputs. They indicate the most efficient physical output that can be obtained from a bundle of physical inputs. They thus reflect one determinant of the cost of a given output. The choice of the bundle of inputs for a given output will also depend on the relative prices of factors.

The production functions above are expressed in very general terms. The character of specific technology is captured by imposing a definite structure on the production function indicating the degree of substitutability between the various inputs and their relation with production including any change with alterations in output scale. Thus, for example, in accounting the technology underlying direct cost is assumed to manifest neither economies or diseconomies of scale.

Later analysis will be applied not only to inputs variable with production and process or activity volumes but will also consider a variety of resource types which are regarded as fixed in both accounting and economics, that is, as not varying with output volume. It is shown that whether items are treated as overheads depend not only on the time period considered but also other characteristics of resources and their prices.

To understand when costs can be treated as direct it necessary to look at several conditions which have to be imposed on technology in order for resources use to be treated as direct with volume. Consideration of how these conditions are infringed by resources not directly variable with output help to indicate the resource characteristics which need to be reflected in accounting if these characteristics are to be portrayed accurately by accounting.

The first two characteristics allow the use of a resource to be treated as independent from both other inputs when considering the outputs of other products and the use of other inputs. This allows resources to be traced to the operations using them without considering other factor requirements within the firm and the outputs of other products.

Here it is being assumed, as is general in economics, that the production function in mind allows substitution between factors. Recently, it has become popular to characterise the production functions underlying direct costs and activity costs as involving Leontief technologies which involve fixed proportions of inputs as exemplified in linear programming. (Christensen and Demski 1995 and Banker and Hughes 1994). The approach adopted here is used because it better illustrates the underlying reasoning. It also recognises that generally in planning the resources being considered are substitutes and that, in this case, the fixed proportions of factors only arise at the stage of production. That is, not all the technologies underlying direct costs considered in planning are intrinsically fixed proportion production processes.

Moreover, even with fixed proportion processes, input substitution can be studied where a given unit output can be produced using weighted average (linear) combinations of two or more fixed proportion processes (Ferguson, pp. 43–46). It can be ventured that Leontief technologies can be taken for practical purposes to satisfy the conditions discussed here (Ferguson, pp. 43 and 50–59) in that the various menus of factors being considered can be determined without considering other products being made and the use of other resources as required by the production function separability assumptions to be considered (see Note 1).

The first two classifications are characterised as follows.

Output Independence

This condition concerns the degree to which the use of a given resource for a specific final or intermediate output (which could be a service rather than a physical commodity) or for the output of a process is fully captured by the ratio of the output obtained by using the resource for one product relatively to the output of another product sacrificed by use on the original product. Its use is otherwise unaffected by the resource demands of the levels of the other outputs and the flow of other services produced by the firm. This characteristic is labelled output separability in economics, see Chambers, 1988, pp. 284–301, where it has a narrower meaning than that being used in this study. What will be called separability here allows total output of a set of multiproduct outputs to be expressed using some type of common index of the volumes of the products, (based, on say, the market prices or marginal costs of the end products of a common factor used by all products). Product separability allows each product to be treated as if it were a separate operation and therefore possessed a separate cost function. Product independence allows each input or bundles of inputs and its product to be treated as independent plants or technologies (strictly it is possible to construct an independent production function for an input (or group of inputs) and its output). This permits the total revenue obtained from a product to be split up and each part assigned to a specific factor (or group of factors). This means that a revenue contribution can be assigned to each unit of a factor used for a given output determined by measuring the change in revenue from a product occasioned by increasing the amount of a factor by one unit.

Thus, with output separability, the resource use of a factor can be traced directly and exclusively to that product. This is a clear requirement if a cost is to be legitimately treated as direct with the volume of a cost object. Another way of looking at product separability is to say that this type of independence exists only where there are no economies or diseconomies of scope, that is there are no cost advantages or disadvantages of producing several outputs together rather than separately. Strict separability means that products are neither complements or substitutes in production. This implies that the usual methods of treating direct costs assume that the technology used does not manifest economies or diseconomies of scope. This may also severely limit the application of ABC in so far as its technological assumptions mirror those of direct costs. For ease of presentation, here the terms separability and independence will be used interchangeably.

Input Independence

This indicates the degree to which the use of a factor is independent of the level of other inputs used in the enterprise. This is called input separability. This allows a separable factor or an independent group of inputs to be treated independently or as an aggregate factor in decision making.

Input separability is concerned with whether the enterprise's overall manufacturing operations can be subdivided into a set of free standing hierarchical operations for each of which an independent production function can be determined in isolation from other volume based operations. Thus in computer manufacture, separate production functions may be independently determined for the operations of making the hard disk and for assembling the computer. Enterprise technology may be so integrated that inputs can not be treated as separable. Generally, a separable technology can be shown to exist where relationship between two separate inputs is fully captured by the rate at which one input can be substituted in production for the other without concern about the level of other factors being used. With the computer manufacture example, this amounts to saying that decisions about resources for hard disk manufacture can be made independently of the amount and mix of the inputs used in assembling computers. Thus, input separability concentrates on independence from other inputs whereas product separability refers to independence from other products. The above discussion may have suggested a similarity between the two concepts. Indeed, it can be shown that under certain conditions the concepts are equivalent (Chambers, 1989, p. 286). However, they both will be used in this study because their different foci are useful in understanding technology and its impact on accounting. There are a number of possible degrees of input separability depending on the assumed character of the independence between factors. These will now be considered.

(i) where the relationship between any two factors used in a sub operation in a process is unaffected by the levels of other factors not used for this task. Here, the overall production function shows the interactive relation between inputs for each separable operation represented by the sub-production functions comprised of the original inputs used for this operation. Thus, where y is final output and $f(x_i)$ represents sub-production functions or aggregates of inputs used for parts of an overall production process, an overall production function comprised of two inputs can be written as:

$$y = F(f(x_1), f(x_2)) \qquad \text{Expression 1}$$

Here, the inputs in $f(x_i)$ can be thought of as producing intermediate outputs which are then used to product a further output via the macro-production function $F(\cdot)$.

(ii) where the relationship between any two factors used in two different tasks is unaffected by the level of resources used in other operations. This yields a production function of the type:

$$y = F(f'(x_1) + f'(x_2)) \qquad \text{Expression II}$$

where the subsidiary production functions, indicated by $f'(x_1)$ and $f'(x_2)$, which are comprised of the original factors, can simply be added together and thus are complete substitutes and

(iii) where the amount of each resource utilised can be treated as not being affected by the levels of other factors. This yields an overall production function composed of the aggregate amount of each of the original factors being used in all the subsidiary production functions so that the overall production function can be written using the aggregates of the original factors ignoring the sub-production functions in which factors are used. Thus, output can be written as a function of labour and material separately where these are the only two factors being utilised (see Chambers, 1985, pp. 41–48).

The importance of the stronger types of input independence is that they apply only to technologies which yield constant returns to scale or to technologies which can be transformed by mathematical operations so that they can be treated as separable in the same way (see Ferguson, 1979, chapter 5 and Chambers 1988 pp. 36–41 and 115–117). Accountants when dealing with direct costs and with activity based costs assume that factors quantities multiplied by their prices can be simply added together. They are thus assuming constant returns to scale. This suggests that, at least, Anglo-Saxon accountants might experiment with more complex technology reflecting non-constant returns to scale.

26

Different types of input separability allow different permissible levels of aggregation. Separability of type (i) above allows the set of inputs within each sub-production function to be treated as if they were one input. Type (ii) allows such aggregates to be simply added together to obtain the overall production function. The final set of sub-production functions allow each original factor in these sub-functions to be totalled across all such functions and the resulting factor sums to be added together in the overall production function.

These two general classifications measure the degree to which a resource can be treated in decision making as independent from other inputs when considering a) outputs of both products and services and processes and b) the level of use of other inputs. For a rigorous treatment, see Blackorby *et al*, 1978, Part I, Kohli, 1983. Separability allows aggregates of inputs and factor prices to be used in decision making rather than having to encompass individually all variables making up the groups of inputs and factor prices.

The two above characteristics are important to accounting because where they are satisfied product or process specific resources can be treated in accounting as independent of both the volume of other products and the use of other resources in the organisation. Satisfaction of these two conditions are important for resources, and therefore costs, to be legitimately traceable to products or processes.

Factor Price Changes

The above analysis has proceeded on the basis of fixed unit prices for inputs because of the wish to concentrate on the impact of technology on accounting. This also seems to be the standard assumption made in the accounting literature and in practice other than for radical changes in factor prices. Few firms change their production methods in the face of factor price changes, at least, in the short run, though some firms, such as oil companies, do have a menu of production functions for different relative input prices. Economists, however, are especially interested in how factor use may respond to relative price changes thus reflecting that the cost function is determined by technology and by factor prices. This section looks briefly at how the incorporation of factor price changes alter the earlier conclusions about how far factor usage can be treated as independent of the usage of other factors. Factor price changes may add a further restriction on when factors can treated as independent of the level of the use of other resources and of production levels. The separability of resources is not necessarily sufficient to allow for a cost function which can be expressed as a function of only factor prices and production volumes.

It was argued earlier that whether resource demands can be unambiguously traced to products or to activities depended upon whether the relevant technology was separable in terms of level of the use of other factors. Separability determines whether groups of factors can be treated independently from other factors. Similarly the components of a cost function in certain situations can be treated as independent of other elements of that function. Cost separability has similar implications for accounting as did technological separability. Generally the conditions for cost separability emphasis different aspects of technology to those associated with technological independence (see Chambers, 1988, pp. 115–117).

Strong cost separability asserts that relative demands for any two groups of factors depends only on prices in these two groups and on output, and hence on technology. Here, the total costs can be obtained by multiplying costs for each group by output (that is, output and factor prices can be considered separately). This is the assumption required for the usual accounting treatment of variable costs and of activity costs which add the cost of sub-activities together to obtain the costs of an overall activity or process. The problem again arises that overall activities cannot be aggregated together unless their outputs are all inputs to a common further activity.

Whether cost functions satisfy the conditions for separability depends not only on the relationship between factor demands and prices but also on the character of the technology used. This is because cost pools $c(y, p_i)$ are a function of both prices (p_i) and production volume (y) which itself reflects the character of the technology being used. Thus, for example, it can be shown that strong cost separability requires that the underlying technology possesses a special character (be homothetic), see Chambers, 1988, pp. 114–115. Similarly, weak separability of the production function (see Expression I) under some conditions is sufficient for the cost function to be separable into sub-cost functions. However, the relationship between product function independence and that of cost functions is not straightforward but different degrees of cost separability imply a variety of conditions for technology. Cost separability generally requires strong conditions to be imposed on the technology employed by the firm. This strengthens the earlier conclusion that the number of factors that can be treated as variable with production or with activities may be very limited. For a more formal treatment of all this, see Chambers, 1988, pp. 105–119 and Christensen and Demski 1995, who have independently stressed the importance of the separability of cost functions in analysing ABC. They do not address in any detail separable technology nor non-volume related activities. The latter authors also consider some of the implications of separable cost functions for the empirical estimation of cost functions and in seeking to test empirically the assumptions of ABC.

Independent Production

This classification really encompasses specific aspects of technological separability discussed above which are of sufficient importance for accounting to be treated as a separate classification. It focuses on whether resources are separable in use for production. At one extreme, a resource may be private in use so that its utilisation affects only the output of the process in which it is being employed and has no effects on the other processes of the firm, other than the forgone benefits consequent on its designated use. At the other extreme, the characteristics of an input may be such that once available, the resource can be used either throughout the organisation or by parts of the organisation without further cost. Such inputs are labelled public inputs indicating that once they are made available for one use, they are simultaneously available for other uses at no or very small additional cost. Indivisible factors where an input must be purchased in discrete units larger than required for current operations may possess these characteristics. Capital resources, such as plant and equipment and land and buildings, with major excess capacity thus may provide familiar examples of resources with public inputs characteristics up to the capacity constraint. Such attributes may be especially likely to apply to resources which are the outputs of intermediate processes, such as a data bank or a personnel manual. Resources may possess elements of both private and public characteristics.

The independent production condition amounts to saying that the resources underlying direct cost must be what are called here private resources. These are resources which are fungible, that is each unit of a given class is seen as being the same in all respects and any unit is a perfect substitute for any other and separable in use whether purchased or manufactured by the firm or are separable in use even though they are the result of a common production process within the firm. Such inputs are unavailable for further use if already planned for use for another purpose (see Hughes and Scheiner, 1980). This is a usual characteristic of resources such as variable materials. In the same way that the consumption of a conventional or normal good removes it from other consumption, utilisation of a unit of material or of a component renders it unavailable for other use. Thus, use of such a resource associates an opportunity cost with its utilisation usually measured by its market price. Such a resource is called a private good. Intermediate resources produced using a common process, the use of which can be traced to the products or activities for which they are used also provide an example of this type of resource.

Inputs that are the output of a common process but which are not separable in use can be called public factors. Common production of computer programmes or software provide an example of this second type of resource. Many resources that are treated as overheads in accounting have this characteristic. Once a resource with this property is created it can be used simultaneously in a number of uses because it is not reduced in quantity by use (see Cohen and Loeb, 1982) and exclusion may be difficult. A data bank is a good example of such a resource as may be a corporate advertising campaign. Many of the resources, the costs of which are conventionally classified as general and administrative costs, also possess this characteristic to a degree. More generally in economics, such resources are called public goods because they are available simultaneously and publicly throughout part or all of the economy (the organisation in our case) and people cannot be excluded from their use such as defence or public television. Although few resources possess only the characteristic of being a public factor, much of modern technology with its emphasis on planning, information and 'know how' which may be made available generally in the organisation is increasing the amount of this type of resource in organisations. The conventional category of joint costs in accounting where a resource produces outputs in fixed proportions provides an extreme example of a factor which has public resource characteristics (see Manes and Cheng, 1988, pp. 1–11).

The importance of public goods in economics is that in general ensuring that their expected costs are planned to be covered requires some deviation from the usual optimal economic decision rules in markets and involves taxing users in some way to reflect the value they assign to the public good (see Atkinson and Stiglitz, 1980, pp. 457–517). However, as will be indicated later, the problem presented by public factors may not be so great for organisations as for the economy in general as the enterprise may be able to exclude potential users more easily than can be done in the economy as a whole. Exclusion may allow the treatment of such resources as if they were private goods. Also such goods may also be routinely available on the market thereby providing an alternative price for users within the firm. (See also Baumol *et al*, 1988, pp. 301–303).

Many fixed resources may manifest strong public good characteristics. Once made available for one use they can be utilised at no cost or relatively low cost in other uses. Similarly, their use for one purpose does not affect their supply for other purposes (at least, up to their capacity level). Generally in economics, it is held that the costs of such resources cannot legitimately assigned to the individual uses of such resources. These are just the costs which accountants have current difficulties in costing. The lack of separability of public factors suggest an additional reason beyond those featured in the accounting literature for expecting overhead allocation to produce distorted costs for decision making and control. Allocations generally will violate the conditions for the various types of separability discussed above. They will generally impose an incorrect technology on many resources as allocation treats resources as if their usage were variable with product volume. The other conditions introduced above will be discussed in more detail in the next section of this chapter and in Chapter 3.

The next part of this chapter looks at accounting for resources variable with output or activities in order to isolate those conditions which do not allow factors described by other technological characteristics to be accounting for in such a straightforward way.

Accounting for Variable Resources

This part of the chapter considers the resource assumptions underlying costs variable with output and costs variable with processes and activities, and costs for constrained resources. One concern with regard to resources variable with output and with process outputs will be to present the conditions under which

Table 1. *Classification of resources by properties of resources which underlie variable costs*

	(A) Operational characteristics	(B) Supply characteristics	(C) Managerial characteristics
(1)	separable in final goods outputs	traded on well organised markets	outputs unambiguous and measurable
(2)	separable in inputs	unconstrained in supply	repetitive in use
(3)	separable in production even if produced or purchased commonly (fungible resources)	possible transaction or switching costs between uses (may apply to all types of resources)	technology understood
(4)	private in use		results of managerial intervention known
(5)	divisible	Example I	
	therefore traceable to outputs	resource assumptions underlying costs variable with production volume	

resources and costs, can be treated as directly traceable to product outputs or processes. These conditions for product outputs are seen to be very restrictive. The same restrictions are seen to also apply to process and activity outputs thereby constraining the application of ABC. This approach (ABC) which deals with some resources and costs which are treated as fixed in conventional accounting is dealt with in some detail later in this chapter, where a number of seemingly new problems with ABC are also considered.

The next chapter deals with resources which are either common or joint and resources which are difficult to manage.

The first set of assumptions shown in Table 1 relate to those resources which are variable with output volume, though variability with process outputs will be considered where affected by the same factors as being discussed.

The classifications used in Table 1 are those introduced earlier in the chapter except that classification 3 (Independent Production) is divided into separability in production (characteristic 3) in Table 1 and private in use (characteristic 4). Columns A, B and C show the assumptions required to describe the characteristics of the resources underlying variable costs under the headings operational characteristics, supply characteristics and managerial characteristics respectively. The required properties for a resource and therefore costs to be able to be treated as variable with output volume are shown in each of the columns. Thus, column A says that such resources should be separable in final goods output (or intermediate goods), separable in inputs, separable in production or on purchase, even if bought commonly with other inputs. It also requires the input to be exhausted by use and be divisible. These requirements are sufficient to allow the use of the resource to be traced to final good output. Column B indicates the requirements that ensure that the resource has a clear market price and column C really reiterates the managerial characteristics already assumed by column A. The aim of the table is to list those characteristics which resources possess if they are to give rise to the usual cost functions describing costs which are direct with volume. This study focuses on operational characteristics. The supply assumptions are required to obtain a definitive price to assign to factors. The various characteristics should be seen as a set of hypotheses concerning the possible characteristics of resources underlying direct costs.

Each of the assumptions in Table 1 will now be discussed commencing with column A (Operational Characteristics).

Operational Characteristics

Resources variable with output and processes

Output separability (1) in Table 1 is necessary to allow different final goods and process outputs to be aggregated as if they were different sized variants of the same product. This means that the underlying technology is of a character that allows the outputs of products, say, products A, B and C to be expressed using a unit of one of products as an index or output measure for the other products. Where this approach is permissible, the volume of a portfolio of products could be measured using units of any of the products as an index to measure overall output. Thus, a portfolio of 1 unit of products A, B and C can be expressed as being equal to 3 units of A where a unit of product A is equal to, say, 1/2 of a unit of B and a unit of C is equal to 1/4 of a unit B and a 1/2 of a unit of A. Output separability therefore allows the use of a single output cost function for both final and intermediate goods. As shown in the table, (1) in column A, this is a required assumption for technology if the costs of resources variable with final goods outputs or process outputs are to be treated as variable costs in accounting. This is because with the usual accounting treatment the variable costs of the output of a product are assumed to be able to be ascertained without considering the level of outputs of other products. Similar comments apply to the costs of activity outputs.

Without output separability, it is impossible to treat products and processes in decision making as independent of other products and processes. In this case, decision making should ideally proceed at the level of product groups or combinations of processes. Thus, the search for independent product or process costs will fail without output separability because the resources used for one product or process will depend on the level of activity with regard to other products or processes where, for example, economies or diseconomies of scope exist or where any type of jointness in production arises.

This problem of the interdependence of the resources required by different products or processes is beginning to recognised in modern accounting where

32

product costs compiled on the assumption of product independence are being abandoned in favour of product group costing which allows the interrelationships between products caused by modern technology to be recognised and made visible. In this setting, conventional product costing which assumes product independence freezes the relationship between products. Such product costs will lose their ability to reflect the underlying technology, where the outputs of other related products affect the product. This suggests that to continue to reflect technology in the face of such changes, budgets should be 'flexed' in a much more refined way so as to reflect the technical relationships between product outputs than is accomplished by just altering budgets for aggregate volume changes without considering the effects of changing the volume of one product on others. The requirements in the second row of the first column of the table will now be considered.

Input Separability

Here, the level of input independence determines the degree to which overall manufacturing operations can be divided into a set of freestanding subsidiary operations, each of which can be taken as having a separate production function which is independent of the level of activity in other operations. The degree of this independence is important for accounting as it helps determine the form of the cost function that can be legitimately used in the face of the firm's technology. Here, the focus of the analysis will be on resources variable with the output of final market goods. As was said above, generally, a separable technology exists when the relationship between any two separate inputs utilised in a production task is fully measured by the rate at which one of these inputs can be substituted for the other without changing output is unaffected by the level of other factors being used in other tasks. Row (2) of column (A) indicates that input separability is required for accounting to treat resource technology as giving rise to costs variable with product output. The possible general forms of independence conditions were discussed in more detail earlier in this chapter. The assumption is that variable costs can be added up using inputs and their prices.

In accounting, it is generally assumed that the resources which give rise to variable costs are separable not only in outputs but also in inputs because variable resources are treated as traceable to outputs in accounting. This is because variable costs for a given product are treated as if they can be added together. This implies that the relevant resources satisfy not only output separability but also input separability of the types listed earlier in this chapter.

These independence requirements make some very strict assumptions about the type of technology used by the enterprise but are necessary to allow the accountant's treatment of variable costs and process variable costs if these are to encompass variations in inputs. Production functions that either yield constant returns to scale or can be mathematically transformed so that the overall production function manifests separability of a type which satisfy these requirements (see Ferguson 1979, chapter 5 and Chambers 1988, pp. 36–41 and 115–117).[1] Such production functions portray technologies which satisfy the usual assumptions made concerning technology which allow costs to be treated as variable with final goods output and activity outputs.

That some production functions manifesting non-constant returns to scale also satisfy the same separability conditions as assumed with variable costs means that factors from some non-constant returns production functions can be treated in the same way as those inputs that satisfy the necessary requirements for factors underlying variable costs. Thus traceability of resources to output does not require constant returns to scale. The production and cost functions associated with non-constant returns will seem more complex than those associated with production functions which display constant returns to scale in the original inputs. As accountants when dealing with direct costs assume that factors quantities multiplied by their prices can simply be added to together,

---

[1]Transforms of a production function convert a production function into another type of function without losing the important characteristics of the original function. It can be shown that for an constant returns to scale production function to reflect the technology which underlies variable cost, which may show returns to scale, the overall production function must satisfy two conditions (Chambers 1988, p. 117). The first condition is that the function must manifest the same degree of scale economies throughout the production function (be homogeneous), that is a given degree of returns to scale (say, increasing returns of the type where a 100 percent increase in all inputs produces a 200 percent in output must displayed throughout the production function). Secondly, the function must be transformation of a function of the type which displays constant returns to scale. Here marginal products will depend only on input proportions and these will be constant on a ray from the origin in an isoquant diagram. Functions with these properties are called homothetic and share the property of homogeneous production functions that the marginal rate of technical substitution between two factors depends only on input proportions and are independent of the scale of production. Leontief production functions are linear homogeneous and it is in this sense they must have similar characteristics to separable production functions. Chambers, 1988, pp. 37–41.

Such transformations may produce revised production functions which are not linear in amounts of the original inputs. Consider a two factor production function of the form $y = A^L K^B$, where L and K represent quantities of the two factors and A is a constant indicating what is called the efficiency of the production function reflecting that output increases for any input bundle as A increases. The superscripts and ß measure the relative intensity of use of the two factors (Ferguson, 1979, pp. 99–100). This function displays constant returns to scale where $\alpha + ß = 1$ and decreasing or increasing returns where $\alpha + ß < 1$ and $\alpha + ß > 1$, respectively (Ferguson, 1979, pp. 165–166). This function can be transformed in a function which displays constant returns to scale.

That some production functions manifesting non-constant returns to scale can be shown to satisfy the same separability conditions as required for variable costs means that such factors have the same properties and can be treated in the same way as those inputs that satisfy the necessary requirements for factors underlying variable costs with constant returns, although the production and cost functions associated with non-constant returns will seem more complex.

Functions that can be transformed in this way possess the property that proportional changes in all factors used in the subsidiary production functions generate the same proportional change in the overall production function (Chambers 1988, pp. 37–41), This allows the behaviour of the overall production function to be captured by adding together the aggregates of the subsidiary production functions. This requires that the rate of substitution between two factors stays constant as the volume of output is increased using a given mix of factors. A second condition requires that the overall production manifests constant returns to scale with respect to the subsidiary production functions.

34

they are assuming constant returns to scale. This suggests another reform to accounting. Accountants should experiment with more complex functions that reflect non-constant returns to scale. Current accounting reports by assuming constant returns in respect of variable costs may be forcing cost behaviour into too simple a model.

Assuming a technology with a linear character, the overall production function implied in accounting can be written as:

$$y = F(f(x_1) + f(x_2) +,...,f(x_m))$$ Expression III

where y on the left hand side stands for final good output and the $f(x_i)$ are subsidiary production functions which contribute to output and x_i is an aggregate measure of the inputs used in each sub-production function. The production function used in accounting displays constant returns to scale. This means that the conventional accounting treatment of variable costs assumes that in the period being considered variable factors will not display increasing or decreasing returns to scale. The character of this assumed technology (it is homothetic where the rate of substitution between inputs is independent of scale, (see Note 1)) means that it also manifests strong independence between resources and therefore the overall production function can be expressed by simply adding together the amount used of each of the original factors. The roles of the remaining characteristics in the first column of the table can be explained as necessary for traceability. If the resource in mind is not private in use or divisible, it cannot be treated as variable with output unless acquired for a specific dedicated purpose as the resource may exhibit some degree of jointness with other products in that it provides services which can be used by other parts of the organisation without cost.

Supply Characteristics

The first two attributes shown in column B of Table 1 are the conditions which are sufficient for resources, not subject to any non-price restraints in their use, to have a clear market price, reflecting the opportunity cost of use. Different types of markets via their price effects may have substantial effect on the amount of resources that can be used. However, these effects will not be considered here except to say that management accounting generally does not specifically report them. The existence of a clear market price where the decision maker is free to use the market, puts a limit on the internal cost that can be assigned to an input. When dealing with more complex resources, using market prices as estimates for the cost of internally provided inputs provides one way of escaping many of the accounting problems associated with costing internally provided resources. The existence of such prices also allows the detection of any cross subsidy in product costing.

The final characteristic of supply attributes refers to switching costs which may apply to any inputs shown in any of the tables. Such costs will not be discussed in detail here as they provide no obvious problems where such switching costs vary proportionally with product volume (or process volumes) (Ferguson, 1979, pp. 204–209) except that in conventional accounting these costs may lose their visibility if treated as overheads. Switching costs not proportional to volume represent costs which may be treated as part of an activity based costing scheme.

Managerial Characteristics

These characteristics are considered because they provide an alternative perspective which helps determine the type of accounting which is feasible for a given type of resource. Costs which are variable with output and which satisfy the earlier conditions said to allow costs to be treated in this way can be managed in a rather different way to those the output of which is fuzzy and ambiguous. Management of variable resources allows the use of fairly programmed decision rules and control techniques. Thus the standard accounting methods for the planning and control of variable resources are very detailed and build in detailed assumptions which are expected to remain stable throughout the planning and control programme. The ability to measure the use of variable resources and to treat their usage as independent of the levels of activity of other products and the amounts of other inputs allow stable standards to be set up in planning and used for control. Characteristics (1), (2) and (3) reiterate assumptions already made. The production function for such inputs cannot be determined without satisfying these three assumptions. That such a production function can be applied implies that the results of managerial intervention must be known (characteristic (4)) and the definition of variable resources imply that such resources are repetitive in use. This last characteristic also facilitates the measurement of resource use.

These are the managerial characteristics that underlie classic accounting planning and control techniques. However, there is one difference between the use of some of these assumptions in accounting and in economics. In accounting, the relationships between resources and their mix are frozen in planning and control at the agreed level for some desired outputs. Changes in inputs prices or supplies are assumed either not to require any changes in input mix or that such changes are not feasible in the time period involved. Where the latter case applies, it is not obvious that conventional accounting signals the need to investigate changes in future periods. In contrast, economics emphasises the trade-off between resources and the need to reexamine previous optimal levels of resources if any variables alter. Input separability does not imply that the trade-off between any two resources is not sensitive to changes in other variables, such as the level of output or resource prices. It merely says that the investigation of such trade-offs can focus only on the resources being considered.

36

An extreme example of the accounting approach is provided by the mix variance where the standard mix is maintained unchanged in the face of alterations in other variables that make necessary optimal changes in resource mix. This neglect of needed changes in the pattern of resource use by accounting in, at least a given period, reiterates the earlier claim that there is a need for accountants and others to investigate the trade-offs between resources. Perhaps ideally, more firms should adopt the policy in planning of devising optimal resource menus to be used, as used for example in catering manufacture, where there are changes in variables to which the pattern of resource usage is especially sensitive. That is, it should be possible to 'flex' plans for items other than output volume changes. These relationships are explored in many Germany companies in order to achieve cost reductions. Similarly, in Japan cost tables are used in cost reduction both in product planning and in the manufacture of existing products. Basically, these tables estimate the sensitivity of product costs under all technologically feasible assumptions, such as different material types, machines and equipment and technologies in general, different product variants, different scheduling assumptions, various lengths of production runs and different mixes of support services or activities (see Yoshikawa *et al*, 1990). Indeed, attention is also paid to improving the underlying production function (Sakurai 1989).

The costs shown in accounting reports in any period generated by conventional management accounting always seem linear, that is, that they take the form

Total Cost $= M(y) + L(y) + V0(y) + FC$ Expression IV

where M, L and V0 and FC represent material, labour costs, variable overheads and fixed costs respectively, and y represents product output. Any cost function frozen at any volume of output will take this form. This does not mean that the underlying cost function is linear once volume or prices are allowed to vary. Taking an economic perspective, interest is directed at how costs will vary as output varies and input mixes changes. To generate linear cost functions, when seen from these perspective, underlying resources must at least satisfy the requirements presented above. It can be argued that management accountants in both the USA and UK do not investigate changes of this type flowing from volume alterations. It is generally assumed that flexing cost functions of the type illustrated in Expression IV for volume is all that is necessary. This approach assumes a linear cost function and a linear type of technology.

The above conditions for resources and their costs to be traceable to units of products are very strong. In the current environment where labour is often not a variable cost, they would seem mainly to apply to bought-in materials, components and services, including utilities. As will be indicated shortly, the same conditions are required to allow costs to be traced to units of process outputs. The restrictiveness of these conditions suggest that few new types of resources and services are likely to satisfy these conditions. This may mean that account-

Table 2. *Variants on the resource assumptions introduced in Table 1*

Variant I: As in Table 1 except:	**Variant II**: As in Table 1 except:
(B)(2) constrained in use; may apply to all other variants	(A)(1) separable only in process outputs (including activity outputs) therefore traceable to processes
Example II resource assumptions underlying variable cost with constrained resources	**Example III** resource assumptions underlying costs variable with process and activity outputs

ants may need to refocus their endeavours away from direct costs if they wish to account for the new resources and services which are emerging in the current commercial environment.

Table 2 presents two variants on Table 1 which are required to describe the resource assumptions underlying a number of other cost categories.

Variant I indicates that the resources underlying costs variable with product volume may be constrained in their supply. Such constraints may also apply to other types of resources. Variant II represents the classical case of ABC where some resources are not separable in final goods or intermediate outputs but are separable in activity outputs. As the characteristics to be used were introduced earlier in some detail the discussion here will be shorter commencing with resources variable with product volume which are restricted in supply.

Limited Variable Inputs (Variant I in Table 2)

Variant I refers to a resource or resources which conform to the assumptions in Table 1 except that they are constrained in supply to a specific amount which cannot be altered in a given period. Such constraints may be associated with all the classes of resources though the results of the other assumptions entertained under the various classifications of inputs may interact differently with any fixed or constrained resources. Thus, the presence of a constrained factor may have different effects under various resource classifications. However, much of the analysis in this section including the basic approach suggested here for dealing with the presence of a fixed amount of one or more resources applies to the other various factor classifications presented and will not be repeated later.

Here what is in mind is that an input which is variable with product output is in limited supply although available in a well organised market because of a managerially imposed constraint or a short term internal inefficiency or market imperfections not reflected in factor prices. Such resources represent a fixed factor equal in size to the stock of the factor. The problems generated by these constraints may be thought of as transitory and therefore not to require much discussion. However, reviewing this setting provides a relatively easy introduction to more complex situations. From an economic perspective, decision making involving fixed factors should proceed by optimising the amount of variable inputs used by minimising the cost of the variable factors used with the constraining factor or factors for each output. Alternatively, the choice of optimal output and product mix with one scarce input can be made using some variant of the familiar procedure of maximising the contribution per unit of the restrictive factor. Ideally, some variant of mathematical programming has to be resorted to where there were several limited factors. The opportunity cost or shadow prices generated by these processes impute the enterprise profits to the scarce resources. These opportunity costs merely summarise optimal decisions and reflect the effect of relaxing each restriction. As such, they are useful for forecasting, for some future decisions that do not change the assumptions used to derive the original decision concerning the optimal combination of resources (more technically, decisions that do not change the basis of the model) and for indicating possible future decisions to augment resources.

Under these conditions, the use of opportunity costs or shadow prices yields other decisions that are consistent with undertaking a full maximisation exercise. Their utilisation in management accounting has therefore often been urged in the literature to charge for the use of scarce resources at their opportunity costs (see Wright, 1964 and Kaplan and Thompson, 1971; Manes and Chang, 1988, urge their use in dealing with joint costs and common costs). This emphasis has decreased over recent years (neither Horngren and Foster, 1991, pp. 762–774 nor Kaplan and Atkinson, 1989, pp. 62–79 discuss either shadow prices or their use in accounting in their treatments of linear programming) reflecting, perhaps, the (seemingly) sophisticated mathematics required and the infrequent use of such methods in practice. The availability of 'user friendly' software packages should have offset the first problem. Additionally, there may be a wish to focus on the basic or primitive decision problem when making decisions rather than use parameters derived from this problem.

As was said above, the economic approach to decision making with fixed resources in the short run is to maximise conditional upon these resources and to treat these resources and their costs as fixed. In the longer term, the approach is to seek that level of fixed resources which minimises the variable costs of the resources combined with the fixed factor for the optimal output in both the short and long runs. This implies that long run and short run costs of all types will be the same where short run capacity of the fixed resource is optimal for the demand being faced. The approach in long run planning is to minimise costs for each output conditional on the amount of the fixed resource and then to choose the optimal amount of the resource that will be fixed in quantity once acquired.

This decision making procedure is used generally in economics to decide on the level of a resource that will be fixed once purchased, such as advertising (an example of what will be called decision driven costs). Here the problem in profit maximising is to choose both the output level and amount of advertising resources that jointly maximise profits. Prior to the period under review, the decision maker selects the level of advertising by solving

$$\text{Max } \pi = f(y, A)$$

where represents profits, y stands for output and A for the level of advertising. Once the decision is made, advertising would be treated as a fixed resource and cost in the period under review and would not figure in any further decision making during the period. This decision making approach would be used with other items that may remain unchanged during the period once decided upon, such as major decisions about production scheduling. This is the way in which resources and costs that do not vary with product volume enter into economic models of the firm. For an example of this reasoning see Alchian, 1959. A similar approach also applies to decision making about discretionary factors that affect the level of resources and costs that are variable with output, such as resources added to each unit of product to achieve desired quality levels.

Thus, during a short run period, the cost of fixed resources only figure in decision making with an economic perspective as an element of that part of total cost which cannot be influenced during the period. However, for the firm to be sustainable in the long run, it must cover these total costs. Thus at times of either the decision to enter or to stay in the business in the long run, both periodic variable costs and fixed costs must be expected to be covered. One way of seeking to achieve this where it is expected that fixed resources will exist is to compute in planning a 'tax' to be periodically levied upon those variable activities which generate revenues in order to recover the fixed costs of the organisation in a way that does not distort the decisions which are feasible in the period being considered. This allows the desired contribution from different activities to be ascertained in a way that is consistent as possible with the original decision model without encountering the problem of arbitrariness associated with overhead allocation (Thomas, 1980) As will be discussed in more detail later, this procedure is suggested as the most economically sensible approach to allowing joint costs to recouped in pricing for public utilities which are subject to price regulation as in the USA (see Brown and Sibley, 1986, pp. 39–58). This approach also seems to be congruent with the practical view that overhead allocation helps to ensure that productive operations bear their share of non-variable costs and serves to remind managers that non-variable costs exist thereby motivating them to obtain value for money from such costs (see Fremgen and Liao, 1981, p. 61, Atkinson, 1987, p. 9 Ramadan, 1989 and Zimmerman, 1979). Overhead allocation based on revenues could be seen as an attempt to levy such a tax.

That in certain cases the treatment of overheads in accounting can be seen as similar to levying a non-distorting 'tax' is a major theme of this study which will be amplified in several further sections. Any such taxes should be of a type which is neutral in terms of long run or short run decisions thereby separating costs from 'taxes'. Such a taxing procedure also satisfies Demski's concern that the need for allocating overheads should not just be imported into the setting being considered but rather should be generated by the decision model being utilised (Demski, 1981, p. 71). Here, the taxes for the use of fixed resources flow from the original decision model and a failure to obtain the planned amount of tax in any period signals the need to reconsider plans. Levying taxes in this way, allows the overall organisational contribution to periodic fixed costs to be dissaggregated to segments of the organisation.

The opportunity costs of fixed and scarce resources discussed above can also be viewed as a tax designed to recover the cost of artificially limited factor. Such opportunity costs are strictly unnecessary for decision making as they relate to a fixed factor which does not need to enter directly into decision making once the size of this stock of fixed resources has been chosen, though they can be very useful in structuring very complex decisions (see Gould, 1962; see also Atkinson, 1983). As these opportunity costs are consistent with the underlying decision model levying taxes based upon them should therefore not distort decisions.

Care is required using this approach as it may overstate the cost of the constrained resource if this is freely available in the market. Where the fixity of the resource is imposed internally, the opportunity cost of the resource measures the profit foregone per unit of the scarce factor because of this constraint and is the responsibility of the decision maker who imposed the constraint. Having stripped out this opportunity cost of the scarce resource, the tax to recover the cost of the constrained but otherwise variable resource would be its market price per unit. Similar reasoning applies where the market imposes temporarily some physical quota on the amount of the resource not affecting prices.

Charging the market price per unit of the scarce resource is consistent with accounting practice (assuming that accounting prices do not deviate substantially from market prices). However, accounting practice seems not to report on constrained factors. Similarly, information on factors in excess supply is not given directly. This suggests that more attention should be focused on these matters in accounting. Excess supply could be signalled in conventional accounts and indeed attempts are often made to measure excess factory capacity (to be considered later). However any foregone profits arising from constrained factors could only be shown as a memorandum entry if it is wished to respect conventional financial accounting principles in management accounting reports. A supplementary approach would be to provide non-financial information on resources either in excess supply or being rationed. With regard to constrained resources, such information might include consequent queues and delays in the plant and any rationing and price premia imposed on customers.

The next section considers resources which are variable with the output of processes including activity based costs, the characteristics of which are shown as Variant II in Table 2.

Process Variable Resources (Variant II in Table 2)

The assumptions required in order to treat resources as variable with the output of processes as distinct from final goods volume are generally the same as needed for product volume related factors as indicated in Table 1. This is not surprising as it is wished to treat the resources in the same way. Many of these common characteristics have been discussed above when introducing each of the characteristics and the logic for these assumptions is the same as used with Table 1. Thus the very restrictive conditions which allow the application of conventional accounting procedures to those resources variable with product output generally apply to process output resources. This finding may limit substantially the wide application of ABC. Thus, it can be said that it is unlikely that these procedures will be able to encompass the characteristics of many of the resources now being used with modern technology. Thus, ABC is not a panacea for all accounting problems. The only difference between resources of the type shown in Table 1 and those covered by Variant II is that the objects to which factors are to be traced are different. Conventional variable resources are being traced to products with Table 1 and factors contributing to processes outputs including activity outputs with Variant II. Thus, all the strengths and weaknesses of the conventional accounting treatment of factors variable with product output apply to ABC.

Activity Based Costing and Resource Use

The above classifications throw light on the resource assumptions of activity based costing (ABC). By definition, ABC assumes that resources are output separable where output is now defined as the output of processes rather than final good output except where activities are volume driven when they would fall to be categorised under Table 1. Similarly, implicit in ABC is an assumption that factors used for activities are input separable.

The overall production function for an activity or process can therefore be written using sub-production functions for each of the detailed activities making up the overall activity. Thus, the overall production function can be written using Expression III as

$$G = F(g(x_1),g(x_2)...,g(x_m)) \qquad \text{Expression V}$$

where G on the left hand side stands for the overall process output and the $g(x_i)$ are sub-activity production functions indicating the output of sub-activities from given efficient bundles of resources. As will be indicated later, ABC employs a linear cost function. Strictly, this means that ABC employs the strongest assumption concerning input separability discussed above where the amount of each factor used in the sub-production functions can be added across all such functions and the usage of each factor is solely dependent on output of the overall activity (G).

Resources which are strongly separable in inputs also satisfy the weaker condition of an additive separable production function. The assumptions about resource separability made by ABC can therefore be usefully illuminated using Expression V. Here the resources used for each sub-operation depend on the output in terms of the activity it generates. This suggests that activity resources and costs are assumed to have the same characteristics as conventional variable costs. This can easily be seen by studying an activity which is output volume related, as are many activities. ABC advocates do not deny that some processes are output related though they tend to emphasis those that are not product volume related. In this case, the above production function would be transformed into the following production function

$$y = F(f(x_1) + f(x_2))$$ Expression VI

This implies that with ABC, resources are assumed to be private. Indeed, it is the essence of ABC to isolate those resources which are separable but are conventionally treated as if they are non-separable by accounting for them as part of conventional fixed overheads. The ABC treatment is legitimate if the resources are separable and fulfil the assumptions for input and activity output separability. The character of the enterprise's technology thus cannot be used to defend allocation in an activity based costing system.

Expression VI also suggests that there is no efficiency reason to maintain activity resource pools for processes which depend on product volume. Such a dependency means that a sub-production function $(g(x_i))$ can be written as a function of product volume (y_i) as $g(x_i)(y)$. Sub-production functions described in this way can be expressed directly as a function only of volume as in Expression VI. Using activity resources pools will do no harm but provides no additional information and may be costly.

Relevancy of Resource Independence to Activity Based Costing

This analysis also indicates that ABC cannot be expected to cope with non-separable resources. This means that ABC would seem to have nothing to say about resources which are fixed or indivisible. Similarly, these assumptions mean that ABC cannot deal with resources with either public good characteristics, including joint resources, or those where the effects of managerial intervention are not clear and the operations involved are ill-defined and non-repetitive.

Expression VI allows more detailed exploration of another problem with ABC which is that activities are not obviously directly related to enterprise cash inflows. Each activity which is not volume related is free standing from any relationship with other enterprise operations which yield present or future net cash flows. That is an ABC cost function only expresses the total cost of an activity and as such does not automatically link costs with revenues. ABC advocates have therefore sought methods of linking activities to those processes in organisations which yield revenues. One method used is seek to first link activities to higher level cost drivers, such as the number of batches and the number of products maintained and second to use those cost drivers to assign activity costs to final cost objects such as products or organisational units. ABC resources and costs represent one element of the incremental resource demands and costs of these final cost objects. They represent general set up resources and their costs (for example, so much per batch of a product) and resources and costs required to maintain the existence of these cost objects (for example, some of the cost of maintaining a product in the firm's product portfolio). Both resource demands and costs will alter with changes in the character of these cost objects. The concern of ABC with incremental resources makes the economies of scale resulting from combining these resources with variable resources more visible than under conventional accounting.

The incremental character of these costs also mean that they cannot be legitimately treated as part of the unit costs of final good products obtained by dividing these costs by product volume, for example, by dividing costs associated with a producing a given batch of a product by the number of units in the batch and by, say, allocating the ordering costs of a batch of components to the individual components in the batch. Many, if not all, ABC studies do this. This is an allocation which yields a constant average cost per unit, which would differ depending on the volume basis used, for example budgeted volume or actual volume and over different batch sizes. The approach can be seen to be even more clearly an allocation where the product in mind consists of two or more variants. This method of attributing costs to product units implies that what commenced as a non-volume based activity finishes being treated as a cost variable with production volume and suggests that varying the volume will change activity costs, for example, batch costs. Such numbers do not measure the opportunity cost of changing batch size or of changing the volume of products within a batch.

Cooper, 1990, distinguishes four levels of activities, unit level (those driven by product volume), batch level, product level (those needed to support the production of a product) and capacity or facility sustaining level. He argues that the first three of these activity costs can be attributed to products and indicates that these are generally assigned to product units in practice in his sample of 51 cost systems. However, he argues that the activities in his fourth level, which are facility level activities, which sustain the general manufacturing process, contain common resources and common costs which can only be allocated arbitrarily, even though in practice some firms in his case studies do allocate these costs (Cooper, 1990, p. 6). Other studies of ABC in practice and other case studies suggest that the assignment of activity costs in all four levels to products generally occurs in practice, at least, in the UK and USA.

44

The correct approach to such resources from an economic perspective and one that reflects their technological characteristics is to consider them in decision making in aggregate at the level of the cost object at which they become incremental. This accords with one of the reforms suggested here which proposes that if problems are experienced in costing at a given level of disaggregation of operations, accounting should be willing to move up to the level of aggregation at which the costs become incremental or direct to the cost object. Thus, decisions should be made at the product level if product unit costs make no economic sense. For some costs, this process may have to be taken further and costs evaluated at the product group level. This is the standard economic approach to these problems and has also been the standard approach urged for use in accounting for decision making. This approach is just another way of saying that decision making concerning resources should occur at that level of the organisation which allows the technology of the resources to be reflected in decision making. Thus the reforms suggested here are consistent with economic theory and some of the accounting literature (but not practice).

Another method of coping with the problem of linking ABC costs to revenue generating operations suggested by those who favour ABC is to seek to distinguish value added from non-value added activities. Such a determination requires linking activity costs with organisational cash flows thereby again introducing volume related factors into activities which are meant to be independent of volume. Strictly, ABC costs can only be charged to the cost object at the level of which these costs become incremental. Such incremental costs cannot be said to yield any specific proportion of the revenue generated by this cost object unless the proportion of this revenue contributed by the consumer in return for the benefits provided by activities can be evaluated.

The incremental nature of many ABC costs causes a problem in estimating the foregone profits flowing from constrained resources discussed above. Using the same argument as above, the market price of resources variable with activity will measure their opportunity costs assuming a well organised market. However, it is not at all clear how the opportunity cost of the constraint on free standing processes and activities can be measured due to the lack of a link between activity resources and profits. In ABC, the link is between the cost object and the aggregate amount of each resource.

Activity Costing and Product Volume

Using the analysis introduced above, it will now be suggested that many ABC activities are often in fact volume related. This means that for some activities the problem of linking activity outputs with the profit generating strategies does not arise though this is achieved by reintroducing product volume into ABC.

As indicated above, the essence of ABC is the categorisation of activity into a number of separate classes depending upon the overall cost driver for each class of activity with each category being assumed to be independent of activity in other classes. Most crucial to ABC is the distinction between volume driven activity and batch driven activity (unit and batch level in Cooper's terminology (1990)) and the treatment of these activities as separable. It is doubtful whether this distinction can always be maintained, at least where volume is substantially variable. A very large change in product volume is likely to require substantial changes in the management of batches. A large increase in volume can be expected to be scheduled in a different way to that required to cope with the previous level of volume. Similarly, a large increase in volume may change the process of ordering material and components. Maintenance schedules and product planning resources may similarly be radically affected by the envisaged level of product volume. Thus, the level of resources and their planned usage may be a function of, at least, large discontinuities in planned or actual product volume.

This possible relation between volume and batch activity has been indirectly analysed in the literature. Alchian (1959) argues that the characteristics of the production process are the rate of output, the total contemplated volume over the production programme, the time span of this programme and the schedule of outputs (the number of batches)in this programme. He, therefore, generally considers how costs would behave if one of these variables was allowed to vary with one or more of the others being held constant. He showed that often changes in one of these variables requires alteration in another variable. He recognised that a larger total volume may require different methods of production, different product support operations and a choice out of a number of production schedules. Schoenfield (1974 and 1990) and other writers on German cost theory have indicated the importance attached to the intimate relation they perceive between volume and other elements of the production programme (see also Gutenberg, 1951 and Heinen, 1983).

One strength of German cost theory is its concern with seeking the optimal way to adjust production operations to planned volume changes out of a possible very large number of different methods of adjusting to such changes, varying from adjusting one factor leaving all others constant to altering all or some factors simultaneously (see Schoenfeld, 1974, pp. 105–110 and pp. 162–66). Exploration of such methods of adjustment convinced these writers that to talk about production volume in a period independently of the effects of other variables was difficult. This lead to the substitution for production volume and other production related variables of the production programme as the overall cost determinant. Production volume emerges as an independent determinant of resource usage only when many other decisions concerning how production should be adjusted to planned volume have been made. Reasoning of this sort allows Schoenfeld (1974) to write that one of the leading authorities on German cost theory, Heinen, said that volume cannot be regarded as a separate independent cost determinant (p. 158, see also Heinen, 1983).

This type of reasoning suggests that production activity is determined by decisions on a large number of factors including

(a)   the intensity of output in the period (volume in the period),
(b)   the volume of production in the production run,
(c)   the overall length of the production run,
(d)   the number of production runs and
(e)   product and model mix.

Together factors (a) to (d) determine the total volume of output over the whole length of the overall production programme and factor (e) determines the mix of this volume. Ideally, the enterprise should optimise all these factors simultaneously in the face of any constraints offered by plant and equipment, manufacturing capacity in general and the resources required to bring about such changes. Such an overall optimisation is necessary because of the interrelationships between these decisions. A change in any decision about one item may change the optimal value of, at least, some other decisions. For example, an alteration in product mix is likely to change the optimal levels of all other items whereas a change in the overall volume in the production programme can be accomplished in a number of ways involving altering the decisions about one or more of the other factors. Decisions of this type will incur different costs in terms of the set up and switching costs for machinery and equipment, supply and logistic costs and planning costs. Trade-offs between the costs of carrying out decisions concerning these factors may also exist. For instance, greater production in a period may reduce set up and switching costs but increase supply and logistic costs. Thus, the division of activities into unit level, batch level and product level is only possible on the assumption that all the above decisions have been made and are likely to remain stable in the future. Otherwise accounting needs to reflect the possible interrelationship between activities of these types depending on the degree of adjustment available to the decision maker. The suggestion that at least batch activities are a function of volume asserts that adjustments between factors (a) to (d) above are always possible and indeed are crucial in optimising the manufacturing process.

In the end, the acceptability of theories about the relationship between the production variables relative to the assumptions of ABC is a matter of obtaining relevant empirical evidence. Some studies in this area are now beginning to be undertaken but little evidence is yet available (Young and Selto 1991, pp. 16–20).

With the view that batch level activities are a function of volume, relevant cost drivers would also be functions of volume. For such activities, the relation between inputs and activity outputs will depend on production volume. That is, the values of cost drivers will vary with production volume. Different values of cost drivers will apply at different production volumes. In contrast, conven-

47

tional cost drivers are either defined with respect to a given volume of output and assumed to be unchanged for usual volumes or the effect of volume on the value of cost drivers is ignored.

Expression VI suggests that to treat all activities other than unit level activities as if they are not a function of volume is likely to distort decision making and control if such figures are used where volume changes are sufficient to change the values of, at least, some other cost drivers. In terms of decision making and control, the underlying similarity of unit level and batch level activities which are affected in some way by volume may be best captured by categorising these types of activities together as, say, production programme costs as suggested by the German cost theory discussed above. Expression VI also indicates that with volume related activities, it is possible to use either activity based costing methods or to work directly with production volume. Using ABC methods here would have an advantage if they lead in practice to a greater understanding of the underlying pattern of resource behaviour than dealing with production volume directly provided that this information was generated at a cost less than the benefits provided.

Thus, the analysis supports those who say that ABC is not a panacea in the sense that ABC can tackle all types of resources. The analysis also suggests one reason why ABC is so appealing to accountants. It allows a new set of costs to be dealt with using the traditional techniques used with variable costs which in general do reflect reasonable assumptions about underlying technology and with which accountants have felt comfortable for a very long time. This allows ABC to strip out of fixed overheads those resources which are variable with activities, thereby treating them in a way that seeks to reflect their technology as suggested here.

The next chapter looks at the characteristics of common and joint resources.

CHAPTER 3

Costs and Technology: Common and Joint Resources

This chapter looks at the resource assumptions of common costs including difficult to manage resources and the technology underlying joint costs. Table 3 deals with common costs as Variant III of the assumptions in Table I and with joint costs as Variant IV.

This chapter first discusses common resources and common costs. The first part discusses various suggested definitions of common and joint costs. The second part presents a fairly extensive discussion of joint costs and their underlying technology. Many suggestions are made for charging for common and joint costs.

Common Resources

With both joint and common costs, it is essential to look at the technology underlying these costs and the uses to which these resources may be put. Focusing only on costs may ignore these influences especially where is often the case common and joint costs are treated as fixed costs which by definition can yield no signals about technology and resource use. This major section concentrates on common resources and the next looks at situations where resources are joint in use in some way.

Before proceeding, it is necessary to indicate the meaning attached to the term common and joint resources as these terms are used in many different ways in various literatures.

Common and Joint Resources: Defined

In the sections dealing with common resources the assumption that inputs are private in use which has so far been made in the analysis is generally maintained and thus usage of the input for one purpose means that it is excluded from another use. All costs of using an input for one purpose are captured by the foregone benefits from not using it for the another purpose. Problems aris-

Table 3. *Common costs and joint costs*

Variant III: As in Table 1 except:	**Variant IV**: As in Table 1 except:
(A)(1)	(A)(1)
common production with and without independence in outputs and inputs; and (A)(3) and (A)(4) resource outputs may be ambiguous and non-measurable therefore non-traceable to processes or final goods outputs; resources may be sunk	not separable in outputs or processes (A)(3) common in production; public in use (includes joint production) (A)(5) may be indivisible therefore not fully traceable to any output or process but may be specific to an organisational unit: cost centre , profit centre, plant, division, group and corporation (C)(1, 2, 3 and 4) outputs ambiguous and difficult to measure, may be non-repetitive in use, technology may be poorly understood and resources may be sunk
Example IV resource assumptions underlying traceable common costs utilising private resources	**Example V** resource assumptions underlying centrally provided services and joint products

ing from any public good characteristics of resources will be dealt with primarily when Variant IV in Table 3 is discussed. Thus in this part, a common resource, (or resources) is seen as a private input (or inputs) which it has been decided to use to produce more than one output in fully variable proportions where the nature of the technology used does not require that the outputs must be of necessity produced together.

Much of the economics literature and some of the accounting literature does not distinguish between common and joint resources and costs. Common resources and costs may therefore encompass an element of jointness between cost objects, such as organisational units or products, where two or more cost objects use the same resources or are the outputs of the same resources (see the discussion in Manes and Cheng, 1988, pp. 1–3). In accounting, a more specific definition of the term common is often used with reference to costs and implicitly also applies to resources. With this approach, common costs are defined as applying 'to a setting in which production costs are defined on a single intermediate product or service which is used by two or more users' (Biddle and Steinberg, 1984, p. 5). In contrast, joint costs 'apply to a setting in which production costs are a non-separable function of the outputs of two or more products' where the products in mind are generally final products (Biddle and Steinberg, 1984, p. 4). Thus, with joint costs, an unavoidable jointness between cost objects is a crucial part of the definition. A more specific definition of joint cost is 'those costs incurred when the production of one product simultaneously and necessarily involves the production of one or more other products' (Hawkins, 1969; quoted and adopted by Manes and Cheng, 1988, p. 2). This jointness in costs is generated by a dependence arising from the technol-

50

ogy used to produce the joint outputs. Hawkins defined common costs as those 'incurred when products can be separately produced with the same or part of the same facilities, but need not necessarily produced together' (quoted in Manes and Cheng, 1988, p. 2). The essence of joint resources and of costs with this view is that two or more outputs of necessity are generated when the resource is used, though the proportion of the outputs produced may vary to a degree.

That the two concepts of common and joint resources and costs are closely related is clear because the Hawkins definition of joint costs would be converted into common costs for some products if it were feasible to allow the proportion of any of these joint products to fall to zero. Thus, one might argue that common costs are joint costs where there is no restriction on the proportions of the outputs produced and the proportion of any product may be zero. This is the definition given by Sharkey, 1982, p. 38. Equally, one could argue that the classic case of a joint cost in accounting where fixed proportions of the outputs are produced is represented by a common cost, the underlying technology of which requires that the cost objects be served in a fixed and rigid proportion.

Much of the literature covering these matters attempt to deal with common and joint resources and costs by converting them into items that can be treated as constrained in supply but variable with process or product outputs so that they fall into the relevant categories above (see Variants I and II) and therefore any jointness disappears. This is achieved by applying mathematical programming methods to these types of inputs and their costs. With suitable assumptions, these exercises yield opportunity costs or shadow prices which may be used to charge common and joint costs to their outputs.

This approach has made many contributions to a variety of problems (see Manes and Cheng, 1988, pp. 14–46 and pp. 137–154). For example, one major contribution in the electricity, telecommunications and similar industries has been to derive 'prices' for the use of capacity in periods of peak and base demand where the capacity is used jointly to supply both demands even where the demands display no clear peak. In this example, if everything proceeds to plan, charging the shadow prices generated by the model for use of optimal capacity in each period plus variable costs to customers will ensure that the marginal investment cost of the capacity will be covered (see Littlechild, 1970 (a) and Atkinson and Scott, 1982, for an accounting application of these results).

These results are volume driven and the shadow prices derived are based upon the forgone revenue resulting because of the existence of capacity constraints. Earlier, it was shown that with activity based costing, some activities cannot be easily associated with product volume other than by using arbitrary allocations. Thus, this approach cannot be used with common fixed resources where an activity based costing system is utilised unless it is possible to express the outputs of different activities using some index.

A necessary assumption for these mathematical methods is that the physical amount of the fixed short run resource or the proportion of the input used by each output is known prior to the commencement of the analysis. This means that extreme separability in products is being assumed in that the amount of resource for a unit of one product is assumed not to be affected by the level of production of the other resource. (Two other ways of saying this are (i) that it is possible to chart the possible transformation between two or more outputs considering separately the resource which in an accounting sense is joint or common and (ii) the amount of the input required can be written as a function of some index of the outputs of two or more goods). A traditional example of a joint cost in accounting is the production from a cow of leather, meat and offal in fixed proportions. This example has been quoted in economics as an example of where the separability of products apply (Chambers, 1988, p. 288). This, perhaps, surprising finding follows from the definition of product separability which say the resources required for a given output, leather, meat or offal in our case, can be determined without considering the level of other outputs. Thus decisions are focusing on only, say, leather production and are independent of the other products. Thus an important finding is that there is nothing *per se* in the character of common costs that means that the inputs that generate these costs and the costs themselves cannot in general be traced to cost objects. (Recall that public resources are not being considered).

Just because outputs are produced in common does not necessarily mean that the resources and costs involved cannot be traced to these outputs. Thus current practice has no difficulty in tracing the costs of fungible components or parts used in common by more than one output to outputs. Similarly, labour used for more than one task in a period can with an appropriate measuring system be traced to the outputs that require these tasks. Thus many items that are treated as common or joint in accounting satisfy the separability conditions shown in Table 1 if suitable measuring systems are used. Thus, for example, there is nothing intrinsic in the character of the utility services used by the firm, such as, electric power and telecommunications, which mean that they cannot be traced to cost objects within firms. It might be suspected that many resources which are treated as joint or common in accounting and therefore included in overheads are in fact traceable. Indeed, the essence of activity costing is to strip out of conventionally defined fixed overheads those resources and costs which are variable with activities.

This, perhaps, esoteric discussion is important to accountants because more and more of the resources and associated costs with which accountants have to deal have characteristics which suggest they are joint or common costs. The standard treatments of these types of resources may not correctly reflect underlying technology which may allow many of these inputs to be treated as variable with product or process outputs. As already stated, there is a substantial theoretical literature utilising mathematically based approaches on common and joint costs (see, for example Biddle and Steinberg, 1984, Manes and

Cheng, 1988 and Weil, 1968) which it will be argued later does not deal completely with the phenomena of jointness. These approaches have not been generally accepted in practice where these costs are generally treated as fixed overheads even though these costs may be of major strategic importance. They may include costs such as planning costs, set up costs, product differentiation cost, quality planning costs, some warranty costs and advertising.

Common Resources Variable with Outputs

To summarise the above discussion in less technical terms and to indicate the concerns of this and later sections, common resources that possess the characteristic of separability in products will be considered in order to further indicate that the frequent treatment of all common costs (and indeed other costs) as if they were fixed overheads is generally incorrect and may produce information that distorts decisions. Resources not possessing public good characteristics, that is, which do not manifest jointness in that sense, which are used to produce in common product or process outputs and which are separable in these outputs and also from other inputs do not fall into this category. Such resources satisfy the conditions said earlier to be required of inputs variable with either product outputs (Table 1 and Variant I) or process outputs (Variant II). Those common inputs which satisfy the above conditions can be treated as variable and traced to product or activity outputs. Conventional accounting includes the costs of many of these types of resources in overheads and misstates their costs by charging them to costs objects using some arbitrary recovery base and which does not reflect their underlying technology.

Variable resources used in common can in principle traced to output. Such tracing should improve decision making assuming that the informational benefits exceed the incremental costs of tracing these costs to outputs. The mathematical methods discussed above go further and transform common resources into resources variable with volume because they assume the amount of the common resource used by a unit of output is known. The total of the charges or taxes (or opportunity costs) based on usage of common factors generated by these models would over the lifetime of the common service equal the present value of the net cash flows generated by the relevant cost objects after meeting variable costs used to justify the acquisition of the common service. This is the case where the assumptions used in planning were sustained when the service was actually in place. Thus, this method of charging overheads is consistent with the original decision and monitoring the scale of these charges against the original plan provides signals useful for future decision making, though, as with traditional overhead variances, much, if not all, this information is available more directly from other sources. Thus the information conveyed by changes in the taxes raised because of alterations from the plan in the volumes of the ultimate products on which the taxes are charged are based is yielded directly by inspection of these volumes and by information concerning capacity use. However, the taxes suggested here value any volume deviation in a way consistent with the original decision model and with opportunity costs providing that there is a perfect market for the common service. Without such a market, the tax should be based on the short run opportunity cost of the common service. This recommended use of opportunity cost does not seem prevalent in practice and without such estimates any tax will not be economically meaningful. It may therefore be better to treat these costs in the short run using the more general approaches suggested below.

Fixed Resources in the Long and Short Runs

There is a relationship between resources in the short and long run which has tended to be ignored by management in practice and explicit consideration of which may help overcome the problem of charging for short term fixed resources without recourse to mathematical methods discussed above. The amount of each type of fixed common resource in a period if it does not exactly satisfy demands in that period will represent either a constraint on feasible operations or over capacity. Thus, the amount of such resources available in a period result from capacity decisions made in earlier periods. The amount provided may be incorrect for the demand faced in the period. Ideally, in a perfect market with resources which can be purchased in divisible amounts, previous decisions should have contributed for any period just that endowment of fixed resource which represents the cost minimising way of producing optimal output for that period. That is, the amount of a fixed resource provided for the period will be just that which would be utilised if it were possible to adjust the amount of resource instantaneously at no adjustment cost to the amount required to produce the optimal output for the period. There, with perfect foresight, the long run capacity and short run capacity of a given resource must coincide. Thus in an ideal world, the demand for fixed resources in any period should just equal the planned capacity of such fixed resources in the period. Thus, with optimal decisions, the optimal amount of capacity should be provided for a period and fixed resources should be used to their planned capacity.

At the point where capacity is optimal for the demand being faced, the long run marginal cost of using the resources must equal the short run marginal cost of use (see Viner, 1931 and Cohen and Cyert 1975, pp. 139–149). The long run marginal cost will equal the alteration in capacity or capital cost plus the change in the long run variable costs generated by a small change in use. Here capacity can be altered because at the time of planning the amount of these resources are variable. In contrast, the short run marginal cost of using the resource will consist only of the variable costs defined on an opportunity cost basis associated with the optimal amount of fixed input without any charge for the fixed resources. Long run and short run marginal costs must therefore be equal if capacity is optimal as both must represent the lowest cost way of producing the desired output. If short run marginal cost exceeds long run marginal cost, this means a larger amount of fixed resources should have been planned to be provided and thus capacity is not optimal for the demand being supplied. Similarly, the amount of fixed capacity resource provided would not be optimal if long run marginal cost is greater than its short run equivalent.

This equality of long run and short run costs where optimal capacity has been obtained represents a very important finding and is relied upon in the peak load pricing studies discussed above where shadow prices or opportunity costs are derived for the use of fixed capacity in different periods. This analysis is based upon the assumption that prices are adjusted so that demand in each period equals the output requirements in each period and that therefore shadow prices will be based on long run costs which include capacity costs (see Littlechild, 1970 (a) and Atkinson and Scott, 1982). This equality allows decision making to be based on either short run costs or on long run costs. Thus in the short run, there is no need for optimal decision making to take into account capacity. If optimal capacity has been achieved, optimal decisions can be made using short run costs. In this setting, exactly the same decisions would be made using correctly defined long run costs including charges for capacity. Thus here, any charge for fixed capacity should be based on its long run marginal cost. However, with this approach variable costs are not those taken from short run accounting reports but those which represent long run variable cost. This analysis allows suitable defined fixed charges based on long run costs to be used in short term decision making (Bromwich 1984, pp. 3–5). This approach would apply with suitable adjustments to resources used for activities and processes.

The above analysis uses long run costs which generally do not appear in accounting reports. However, accountants can provide useful information about the capacity balance of the firm which would be useful for capacity decisions. Evidence of inputs either acting as constraints on output or of idle capacity signal that planned capacity is not optimal for the demand being faced and that new capacity decisions may need to be taken depending on expected future demand and on the presence of any capacity indivisibilities. Conventional accounting reports say little about capacity constraints. Thus one reform to accounting reports is to provide information about constraints on production. From an economic perspective the cost of such constraints should be quantified ideally by valuing constrained resources at their opportunity costs or shadow prices, which are familiar from linear programming exercises, such as those discussed above. These measure the increase in net revenue flowing from relaxing a constraint by one unit. As has been said already, such calculations are probably beyond the accounting technology of many firms, but by no means all, as they involve access to a mathematical programming model of the relevant segment of the organisation. Two more practical solutions are to value any foregone sales at the contribution yielded by the products generated by the resource (revenue less relevant incremental costs) or to undertake *ad hoc* studies using the usual financial modelling methods to ascertain the net revenue lost because of the existence of a constrained input. With the former measure, adjustment is needed where the revenue lost because of a constraint can be made up in late periods. The net value of such later production needs to be deducted from the contribution lost in the period in mind because of the constraint.

If none of these solutions are feasible, non-financial information concerning constrained resources may be included in regular management accounting reports. The supplementation of accounting reports by the provision of non-financial information which provides information which not given in an accounting format is a major theme of this report.

Similar considerations apply to information concerning under utilised resources. Idle time measures and capacity variances are thus perhaps more useful than is generally thought. The capacity variances in mind differ from conventional variances of this type as these generally embody arbitrary overhead allocations which have no economic meaning. The economically correct valuation of such variances is very sensitive to the setting involved.

An example of the simplest setting is where the excess capacity cannot be used in the organisation in later periods nor can it be sold on the market. Here the excess capacity has no opportunity cost other than any costs rendered necessary by maintenance of the excess capacity. Such excess capacity represents a sunk cost. Here an economically orientated variance would compare any incremental costs associated with the capacity including those required to maintain the capacity (such costs may be negligible because all such costs may be joint with the total capacity) with the cost of disposing of this capacity or of being released from any commitments which provide the excess capacity. Where later use opportunities within the firm are expected to arise, the cost of excess capacity is again the cost of maintaining this capacity until required for use plus the net of the discounted savings in future user cost less the cost of disposing of this excess capacity. A slightly more complex setting is where any excess capacity cannot be used in the organisation in later periods but can be sold on the market which implies that such excess capacity does not arise from, at least, imperfections in the second hand market. Here, the foregone revenue from maintaining the excess capacity is measured by the net receipts from any sale.

The remainder of this part looks at the problems that arise with common resources when they are neither separable in outputs nor inputs or where their outputs are difficult to define commencing with non-independence in outputs.

Common Resources and Non-Independence of Outputs

Here, the amount of resource used for one output depends on the level of other outputs, that is, the technological relationship between the products manifest jointness. Such problems may arise because of the presence of economies of scope and are generated by the presence of public goods and resource indivisibilities and therefore may merge with the final type of resource to be considered. Such problems also arise from the relationships of production outputs where the outputs are dissimilar and their outputs cannot be expressed using a common index. Thus, in this situation, there exists no obvious basis on which to charge common costs to products. Similar problems may exist with activities in activity based costing. However, in theory, ABC only considers those inputs and their costs which can be traced to activities and does not seek to encompass seemingly non-traceable common or joint resources.

However, there may be ways of overcoming these problems some of which will be dealt with more fully in dealing with Variant IV below. It may be possible in an organisation to exclude an organisational segment from enjoying the output of the common resources. The amount that such an excluded part of the organisation would be willing to pay for the input yields some evidence of the value of that common input to that organisational unit. With a fixed common resource such a valuation does not measure the cost of servicing the unit. Rather, it indicates the amount that the organisational segment would be willing to bear as a tax to recover the cost of the common fixed resource.

The maximum tax on the common resource to an organisational unit should not be greater than the lower of either the market cost of the service if it were to be obtained by the unit on a stand alone basis or the minimum cost of the service to the unit if it were to obtain the service on the market in coalition with one or more organisational units. This assumes that the provision of the common service has no effects on the organisation which are not captured in market prices. That is, the resources involved are not joint with other inputs in the firm and their use has no indirect effects on other areas of the firm. Where the common resource is private in use, any tax can be levied as a charge per unit of service.

With non-separability in products, there are two other important economic meaningful approaches to common costs. The first of these is to treat common resources and their costs as suggested for joint resources and costs below. The other method is to charge the cost as a fixed charge to the aggregate of the profits from all products or cost objects using the common service and not to seek to allocate this charge over product units. This is an application of an approach often suggested here. Where charges to individual products or organisational units are not economically meaningful, the aim should be to ascend the product or organisational hierarchy until a level is reached such that the resource use and total cost becomes incremental to some product portfolio or set of processes or organisational units. This accords with German management accounting practice where contributions (revenues less incremental costs) are often calculated for orders, for products, for product groups and for each of a hierarchy of organisational units (for a treatment in English, see Strange 1991a). Thus, in Germany and a number of other countries, contribution analysis is used much more extensively than in Anglo Saxon countries to provide a hierarchy of contributions both for products and organisational units.

Thus considering products as an example, the approach suggested here is that the cost of common resources with non-separable products should be charged as a lump sum tax to the aggregate of all the cost objects which use the services of the common resources. As the charge represents a lump sum, it will not distort long run or short run decisions. This tax would measure the incremental opportunity cost of rendering the service providing that the periodic cost of the resource measures the fall in the economic value of using the service during the period—the user cost. Estimates of user costs measure the consumption of the service and are only equal to accounting costs by chance, at least, in the short run where capacity is not adjusted optimally to demand. In the short run, any tax for a common service has to be treated as fixed because without product independence common costs should not be used in short term decision making.

Common Resources: Outputs Ambiguous and Non-Measurable

This setting in general refers to a classical case where overhead allocation is resorted to in practice because resources and costs are not otherwise traceable to either the output of goods or of processes. So far the analysis has generally assumed that resources, their underlying technology and outputs and their management are all completely defined. However, in practice, many resources are treated as overheads because these characteristics are absent and because many transactions giving rise to costs are one off thereby inhibiting learning about their attributes. Hofstede (1981) has categorised these problems in terms of the difficulties they present to management in terms of planning and control. So far we have been generally dealing with resources that have the following characteristics:

(a) have clearly measurable outputs from repetitive operations which can be stored if not used during the period and which are tradable on well organised markets and
(b) possess an underlying technology which is well understood and therefore the potential effects of any managerial intervention on resource usage are clear. These are the conditions put forward by Hofstede for inputs susceptible to what he calls routine and expert control which includes accounting and economic control of the type that has figured above. Expert control is used where activities in the firm are one-off but the procedures to be used are well known to trained experts.

Thus much of accounting for the above type of resources is fairly routine in its exercise. However, the effects of managerial intervention may not be known because full details of the technology are not clear in the sense that inputs and outputs are unable to be fully related. Here, control by trail and error may be used where learning is possible and intuitive control used with one-off activities. Thus, these resources and their costs are amenable to the economic and accounting planning and control techniques discussed above.

The resources in the category considered in this section do not have these attributes. Rather they can be characterised in the following way:

(a) having only ambiguous outputs which are difficult to define and quantify and to link empirically to enterprise objectives. These outputs may appear simultaneously with production, are simultaneously available for a number of uses, are not storable nor tradable on well organised markets and may result from one-off operations and

(b) the potential effects of managerial interventions are obscure, because the underlying technology is not well understood, with debateable consequences and the inputs are used for ill defined operations.

Resources with these characteristics may not be traceable to the outputs of processes utilising them and may be traceable only to the organisational unit in which they originate. Such factors thus have many of the familiar characteristics of resources which form the some of the most difficult overhead categories with which accountants have to deal.

Here, Hofstede would expect the use of judgemental and political control. Political control requires that bargaining and consensus seeking activities reflecting power structures are undertaken to resolve ambiguities between resource objectives, to solve the distribution of resources problem and deal with conflicting values within the organisation. Given these difficulties, one possible approach for the accountant is to seek to convert resources of this type into those which are more amenable to accounting control by investigating the underlying characteristics of resources to ensure that they cannot be converted into resources of the other types considered in this and the previous chapter in the same way that ABC allowed some resources which were conventionally treated as fixed overheads to be converted into those that varied with activities. Similarly, many of these resources may represent discretionary inputs and may therefore be related to their expected and actual impacts on the market.

All resources are used for something and should be able to be linked with at least their intermediate output even if they cannot be related to a final organisational objective. This linking of resources and intermediate outputs may not be possible using accounting numbers and may require the use of non-financial output measures in planning relating expected resource use to expected outputs over a planned time schedule including milestones and critical events. Similarly, control may be exercised using non-financial performance measures. Thus one way to approach the problems raised in this section is to use a variety of non-financial performance measures. Such measures are as yet little used by accountants and clearly are not necessarily owned by them. However, there is a need to ensure that the accounting system and any information system using non-financial signals either provide consistent signals or the outputs of both information systems are available to decision makers. The use of non-financial indicators may not ensure optimality where they cannot be linked to ultimate organisational objects and where therefore the trade offs between performance measures cannot be quantified.

Another way to seek to gain an understanding of the input/output relationships in which such resources are involved is to move up the organisational hierarchy. Often any ambiguity as to the output of an organisational unit when considered at one organisational level is resolved when considered at a higher level. For example, at the level of the cost centre, outputs cannot be measured in money terms but they can be so measured as part of the resources employed by the profit centres to which they contribute. Outputs and inputs can be related at this organisational level. This relation at the profit centre level may be difficult to disaggregate to cost centres by the use of transfer prices for exchanges between the cost centres, and the profit centre without a perfect market for the physical output of the cost centres and a production process which is separable in inputs and in production. If these conditions do not apply, planning and control at the cost centre level may have to use non-financial measures to quantify output. For many what might be called expense centres, such as the legal and public relations departments the outputs to which they contribute may be made no clearer by ascending the organisational hierarchy. However, the cost object with which such centres are associated can be determined by continuing the process until that organisational level is reached where the resources are deemed avoidable with its closure. The full cost of the process can therefore be charged to that organisational unit. For many processes of this type, their resources will only become avoidable at the level of the organisation as a whole. Moreover, that an economically rational cost object can be found does not mean that the efficiency of the level of services can be judged because the relation between the services and the output of the cost object may remain ambiguous.

Hofstede and many other organisational researchers would suggest that any methods which attempt to convert resources with ambiguous and difficult to measure outputs into resources categories which are easier to manage must be treated with care. They believe that many of the procedures advocated for doing this in a wholesale way in the past have failed and similar attempts will fail in the future. They see many organisational processes as intrinsically ambiguous and handleable only by judgemental and political processes within the organisation. Hofstede (1981) is scathing about the Program Planning Budgeting System (PPB(S)), Management By Objectives (MBO) and Zero Based Budgeting (ZBB) for this and other reasons (see also Jablonsky and Dirsmith, 1978 and Wildavsky, 1975).

As was indicated above, many of the problems disappear if the output of the resources used for these types of activities are available on the market. Such market prices measure the opportunity cost of the internal provision of the activity and gives an external valuation of these activities. The existence of such a market price provides a external cost for the activities which may be more useful in decision making than treating these costs as a fixed cost to be allocated in some way. Market availability should also open up the possibility of using expert control for these resources and their costs by utilising experts in the provision of the relevant service who through a varied experience of the provision of the service have gained an understanding of the underlying technology.

Several methods for seeking to reduce the incidence of resources with ambiguous and immeasurable outputs have been suggested above. However, resources of this type will always exist which cannot be rendered more easier to manage. Indeed, it might be suspected that their incidence will increase with time as society and industry experience further complexity. The costs of such resources should be traced to the cost object which accounts for their existence, even if this is the firm itself. Attempts to allocate them with other fixed costs should be resisted. Such allocations imply a known technology for such resources where none exists. However, the total costs of these resources have to be met if the organisation is to be sustained in the long run. Any charge to organisational units for such resources should be in the nature of a tax of the form which produces the least distortion in planning and control for the organisational unit that bears these costs which thus should not enter into decision making.

This is the same conclusion suggested for the last resource type to be considered that of public goods which will be discussed in the next section. It will be seen that the inputs discussed in the present section share at least some of the characteristics of public goods and thus the two resources classifications at least overlap if not merge. Prior to discussing joint resources, the next two sections focus briefly on two types of costs which may fall within the category of difficult to manage resources.

Decision Driven Costs

These resources, may apply to all cost categories in the accounting literature. The costs of these resources feature in management accounting textbooks but generally have been accorded a brief treatment often involving an implicit admission that accounting can be of little help with these costs in decision making and that they are capable of accounting control only in the aggregate and often in rudimentary ways. A superior, though short, presentation is Kaplan and Atkinson, 1989, pp. 29, 193 and 531. A fairly comprehensive treatment is contained in Horngren and Foster 1991, pp. 432–443.

In the accounting literature, these type of resources and their costs are generally held to have at least three important features. The first is that they arise from periodic decisions usually in yearly budgeting and programmes for expenditure are committed until decisions are revised or agreed commitments cease. The second is that their link with corporate objectives is often not clear and no clear relationship exists between outputs and inputs (normally mainly labour) because the underlying technology is not well understood which makes difficult predictions of the effects of managerial intervention. Finally, many discretionary costs are seen as the result of a portfolio of one-off and ill-defined activities. These assumptions concerning discretionary costs places them firmly in category mentioned above which describes resources which are difficult to manage. Examples of decision driven costs often given include advertising, public relations, training, research and development, health care and some activities of general and administrative departments such as accounting, industrial relations and human resources.

Few attempts have been made to define decision driven costs. A definition which can be applied to these resources and can be expanded and stated in more technical terms is as follows:

> Decision driven resources are those which are not technologically determined in that they are not essential to the production of either product or process outputs, where a essential input is one of which a positive amount must be possessed if the production of output is also to be positive.

The essence of discretionary resources is that their amount is not determined by the production technology used by the organisation but rather by managerial decisions. This suggests their planning and control may take a different form to technological determined resources. It also suggests that the treatment of their costs as fixed and their allocation as part of these costs confuses them with other types of costs and renders invisible any special characteristics possessed.

The above definition suggests that many resources and their associated costs that are conventionally treated as discretionary do not fall into this category. This is especially important because it is often said that conventionally defined discretionary costs represent an increasing proportion of overall costs.

The familiar descriptions of discretionary costs are very wide and may include resources and costs which possess, at least, some characteristics of the other types of resources discussed here and their associated costs. While it may be generally the case that discretionary resources are not product volume related, many clearly contribute to processes and activities. Other discretionary resources represent, in part, set-up and infrastructure costs, that is, they are similar to many other fixed resources employed by the enterprise.

Entertaining the above definition and focusing only on costs of resources correctly described as decision driven suggests that it is difficult to understand why such resources would be employed by a profit maximising firm. However, it can be suggested that many discretionary costs should be appraised in terms of the benefits they provide to consumers and for which the consumers are willing to pay (Bromwich, 1990). This approach helps provide the missing link between inputs and outputs for many processes which are generally treated as discretionary and provides a way of understanding the contribution of decision driven resources to the organisation. Thus, at least, some types of discretionary resources are employed to either maintain demand in the face of competition or to increase demand. With this approach, the benefits provided by products which generate enterprise revenues are seen as the ultimate cost drivers. From a strategic perspective, this category of cost drivers dominate those cost drivers used in traditional accounting and in activity costing when, as seems to be often the case, this approach is used in a routine way to attribute costs to products and not to the benefits which the activities represented by these costs provide to the consumer.

With the most general customer value perspective, each resource possessed by the enterprise is seen as being able to be linked to providing customer benefits which help meet the needs of customers (except for some resources which are incurred to meet regulations imposed by authorities external to the firm). What is called strategic cost analysis allows the costs of these resources to be integrated with operational plans because it seems to make the links between costs and the customer benefits they provide visible to management at the operational level. With this approach, the utility of training costs, for example, becomes much more transparent. Here training should be carried out only if it provides specific benefits to customers for which they are willing to pay more than the consequent costs of these benefits. This test can be applied to training decisions at all levels in the organisation thereby allowing the integration of the strategic benefits of training into operational plans. It has always been impossible to provide this integration within in conventional management accounting where strategic planning activities, more generally, had to be decoupled from current operations because accounting systems report only the costs of enterprise current operations.

With this customer value perspective, an approach to understanding decision driven resources and their costs is to see products not as comprising of a whole but as being comprised of a package of objective attributes or characteristics which they offer to consumers (Lancaster, 1979, pp. 16–36). It is these attributes that are seen as actually constituting commodities and appealing to consumers. Demands for goods are, thus, derived demands stemming from their underlying characteristics. These attributes might include a variety of quality elements, such as operating performance variables, reliability and warranty arrangements, physical items, including the degree of finish and trim, and service factors like the assurance of supply and of after sales service. (Lancaster, 1979, pp. 27–28 and Shaked and Sutton, 1986a, pp. 107–108). It is these elements which differentiate products and appeal to consumers. The firm's market share depends on the match between the attributes provided by its products and consumers' tastes and on the supply of these attributes by competitors. The focus of the analysis here is on what is called "horizontal product differentiation" in economics.

With the customer value perspective approach, many decision driven resources are seen as required in order to generate product attributes, that is they provide characteristics of the product which attract consumers and for which they are willing to pay. Thus, for example, decisions on product quality lead to the institution of processes which seek to guarantee a desired level of quality. These processes can be evaluated and monitored by comparing the costs of the resources used with the amount consumers are willing to pay for the outputs of these products. This linking of decision driven costs with the product attributes they generate and the revenues thereby obtained, yields a way to tackle some of the resources and costs which accountants and managers find difficult to handle.

Relating the output of decision driven processes to the market benefits they provide allows strategy to be driven down the organisation. The output of each process in terms of market benefits provided can be related to the resources employed to achieve these benefits and the costs of these resources. This approach may be especially helpful for understanding decision driven decisions seemingly far removed from attracting the consumer. Additional administrative or central resources can also be appraised in this way by linking these resources with the increase in customer benefits believed to be provided. Decision driven resources are thus seen as being used in processes which are market related and can be appraised in this way.

In practice, the costs of decision driven resources would be treated by placing them into the appropriate cost categories. Thus, the costs of quality related decisions which affect direct product costs may be treated as if they were variable costs. Similarly, the cost of capital resources required to obtain a desired level of quality would be treated as other capital costs.

However, this method of cost categorisation ignores the special characteristics of, at least, some of these resources which is that their usage and costs depend on decisions made in order to affect the level of market demand. Here, the responsible decision maker should regularly receive reports that indicate how the fruits of their decisions compare with expectations at the time of decision. This suggested approach represents an important reform to accounting which tends to ignore decision driven resources and where it does consider them, it tends to focus on their costs and not upon their impact on the market. The conventional accounting categorisation of discretionary resources and costs also ignores the property that the amount of these resources may be changed more easily than other inputs which are technologically determined.

Not all discretionary costs can be dealt with in the way suggested above though the scope of this approach is wider than might be thought. Some advertising can be thought of as providing information, entertainment to the consumer and improving the perceived status of the product in society and therefore to the consumer. Indeed, Horngren and Foster (1991, pp. 432–445) generally discuss discretionary costs as if they satisfy the properties listed at the beginning of the previous section and emphasise their indirect link with corpo-

64

rate objectives and the ill-defined nature of discretionary activities. If this is the case, they fall into category of resources that are difficult to manage. Many discretionary processes can, however, be treated using activity based costing and activity based management. Similarly, the control of decision driven costs may lend itself to using non-financial indicators, where the nature of the processes can be defined in these terms, if not in financial terms. These approaches do not solve any problem arising from any possible ill-defined link between decision driven activities and corporate objectives. This is because both of these approaches treat the activities involved as separate processes and use measures not clearly linked to the enterprise's cashflows and objectives.

Regulatory Resources

The second difficult to manage category is one which does not generally figure in accounting. It encompasses all those resources within the firm which are devoted to satisfying regulatory requirements. Such resources may fall into any of the usual categories. Thus, some health and safety regulations may effect indirect labour, and the type of resources that are used to produce units of output but most regulations affect equipment and capital resources. Regulatory requirements are wide ranging and may affect many corporate activities. Thus, for example, the accounting department has to respond to a very wide range of regulatory requirements including the collection of taxes, preparing statutory accounting reports and following accounting standards.

Regulatory Requirements Which Impose Variable Costs

Few management accounting reports delineate the costs of such activities separately. This may be because the characteristics of the costs associated with these resources make them indistinguishable from other costs with the same characteristics. Thus, say, variable product costs required by health regulations are in many ways indistinguishable from other variable product costs. Similarly, activities or process related costs imposed by regulation generally can be treated in the same way as other process costs and be charged to the cost object requiring the process activity. Such variable costs may be able to be designed out of the cost object in the same way as other product variable or process cost. However, it is important to understand the usage of such resources is not technologically determined but rather represents costs imposed at the discretion of others. Such requirements may be thought of as of two types. Those which the company can only avoid by ceasing production or the process with which the regulation is associated, such as specifically defined items as safety requirements on vehicles, such as the requirement for safety belts and anti pollution devices on cars. Those to which the firm can respond in some way, by phasing out the use of a regulated material, component or operation. At the extreme, production may be moved to other countries in order to escape requirements including social security and pension requirements. For planning purposes, it may be useful to report separately these two types of costs especially as the definition of inescapable regulatory requirements indicate they have a characteristic which is normally associated with fixed costs, they cannot be avoided if production is positive.

Joint Resources

Table 3 (second and third columns) introduce the final variant on the our original assumptions (Variant IV) and assumes that either resources themselves are public goods or the output of the use of resources is a public good. As such, the cost of the resources cannot be traced to the consumption of the output by any specific organisational constituent. Resources which themselves are public goods or which generate public goods are traceable only if they are provided for a given organisational unit, such as a cost centre, plant or division and are not available to other units.

Variant IV addresses some very complicated settings. Here, resources are not separable in final good or intermediate good outputs or in process outputs. All outputs are produced in common and these outputs themselves or the resources used to produce them have public good characteristics and may also therefore be indivisible. Thus, this variant allows for jointness in production between outputs and permits resources to have a public good dimension. By their nature, such outputs may be ambiguous and difficult to measure and their underlying technology may not be well understood. The costs of such outputs and resources may be difficult to trace other than to the organisational units which require their use and which cannot be excluded from their use. Thus capacity inputs, such as storage space used by only one plant can be traced to that plant. Similarly, resource usage in maintaining a data base required by only one division can be traced to that division. Many resources of this type are sited at the division, group and corporate level therefore and cannot be further traced down the organisation. Resources in this category may also have the characteristics of sunk resources because their nature makes them difficult to market.

Thus, this class of inputs generates many of the most difficult problems accountants have to solve. This class of resources pervades the organisation and represents a major category of resources which is perhaps, not well handled in accounting. An essential characteristic of these resources is that they provide capacity which generally has to be provided in discrete units and the cost of which generally represents a lump sum investment or commitment incurred prior to any usage. The capacity provided is the facility to yield services when required. Another essential property of such resources is that they are generally not exhausted by use. The ability to provide basic research services provides an example.

That these resources involve providing capacity rather than inputs which are used up directly in production leads to a major suggestion of this study which is substantially at variance with conventional management accounting. This is that capacity providing resources and their associated costs should be accounted for in a way reflects both capacity provision and the public good characteristics of such resources. Much of the remainder of this study is geared to suggesting how this might be achieved. Studying the underlying resource characteristics indicates that many of these problems originate in the technology underlying costs and not just in accounting. This suggests that accounting solutions that do not respect the underlying technology are unlikely to be helpful in decision making. Allocating the costs of such resources is tantamount to treating them as costs variable with outputs or processes and therefore distorts the underlying technology.

Although resources with these types of character seem complicated, they may be encountered at all levels of the organisation. For example, equipment with spare capacity provides an example of a public good encountered at a fairly low level in the organisation. Information systems at all levels in the organisation may have some of these characteristics. Thus conventional accounting applied to such resources may distort costs away from the underlying technology at very basic organisational levels. These problems do not arise only in charging out corporate services to divisions which seems to be the level at which these problems are often considered in the accounting literature. Many public type inputs are found within individual organisational units or are shared between groups of units. Moreover, modern technology including information technology seem to be increasing the proportion that these types of resources form of enterprise resources. These are just the type of inputs the accounting for which is generally held to cause the most problems. Many of these, especially those provided at group or corporate level, may be discretionary or decision driven. The earlier analysis of this type of cost should help in at least valuing these resources for the user. Arriving at such values has been a major problem in the literature. In the accounting literature very few articles have considered resources with public good characteristics (see Cohen and Loeb, 1982, for the major contribution).

Resources with Public Goods Characteristics

The essence of a resource with public good characteristics is that of jointness in use. That is, the benefits from the input may be conferred generally and ,perhaps, indiscriminately within the firm. Corporate advertising provides an example. Once the advertising decision is made, some set of organisational units within the organisation or all parts of the organisation gain the benefits of such advertising. Similarly, the resources underlying a joint cost process which automatically supply benefits to more than one product or department simultaneously provide examples of public resources.

The cost structure of a public resource or service will generally resemble that associated with fixed costs where the initial supply requires a large outlay and the supply of the resource or service has a zero or very low marginal cost. Resources which have the characteristics of public goods are supplied jointly to more than one user and employment by one part of the firm does not reduce the supply to other users (Samuelson 1954 and 1969). Use of an existing data bank would provide an example. The possibility of several products being allowed to use any substantial excess production capacity may provide another example. As may the use of the same capacity for different demands over time, such as supplying peak and off-peak demands and the use of a given capacity in providing different services where capacity may be regarded as infinite as with some elements of a telephone network. This characteristic is called non-rivalry in use or non-depletability. This attribute does not apply in the case of a conventional good, such as a unit of raw material, where usage for one purpose denies use for any other purpose. A second characteristic of public goods is that of non-exclusion. This means in the context of the firm that organisational units cannot be excluded from the enjoyment of the resource or service. A corporate-wide credit ranking provides a good example. It is impossible to exclude any part of the organisation generally identified with the corporation from enjoying any benefits flowing from such a credit ranking. Similarly, it may be impossible to avoid the firm's reputation being exploited by individual organisational units. For a general review of the characteristics and properties of public goods in economics, see Atkinson and Stiglitz (1980), pp. 482–518.

Generally, it is argued in economics that commodities rather than being pure public goods may manifest only some of the characteristics of public goods. The existence of a pure public good would strictly require that the good provides simultaneously the same physical service to all users and that no one can be excluded nor can exclude themselves from the enjoyment of such services. The non-exclusion assumption may well not apply in organisations where potential users may often be able to be excluded by management decree or sufficiently ingenious administrative arrangements. It may however be difficult for organisational units to exclude themselves without corporate agreement. Many firms require that their organisational units use services provided by the firm rather than opting out of any provision or purchasing supplies on the market. This often seems to be the case for services provided at group or corporate level. Such services may thus have public good characteristics. Both excludability and jointness are only fully technologically determined for a pure public good. Thus, pure supply jointness requires that the marginal cost of supplying the resource or service is zero and the marginal cost of utilising the resource or service once supplied is zero.

Marginal costs may however be relatively low for inputs with public characteristics and the public nature of such a resource may therefore be expected to dominate those it possesses in common with conventional inputs. The inability to exclude can be argued to be unlikely to be fully technologically determined. Within the firm, organisational units may be excluded, at least partially, by managerial power, administrative decree, levying access fees, by monitoring usage and various physical or electronic entry limiting devices (such as, authorisation codes required to obtain access to restricted information in an information system). The scope for the employment of these devices may quite large within firms (see Baumol and Ordover, 1977).

The importance of public goods in economics in general is that their provision cannot be easily handled by the market because enterprises will only supply the market with public goods if they are allowed to exploit their monopoly power in order to cover average costs given a cost structure that manifests economies of scale (strictly, subadditivity which requires that the cost of producing in one production unit is less than producing in two or more units; see Baumol et al, 1988, p. 19). Thus some deviation from the usual optimal rules of economics is required in order to allow firms to cover costs. Alternatively, public goods will be provided by the government. Government provision ideally involves seeking to tax users in a way that reflects the value they place upon the public good (Atkinson and Stiglitz, pp. 457–517). Practical problems arise here because consumers will seek to free ride on the provision financed by others by misstating their willingness to pay for any public good. Similar problems may be encountered in firms in trying to get organisational units to indicate their willingness to pay for joint services. Such problems are diminished for firms to the degree that the centre has an extensive knowledge of the demands of subordinate units.

One popular approach to common and joint costs in the accounting literature, if not in practice, was discussed above in the section entitled Common and Joint Resources Defined. This involves using mathematical programming models to derive shadow prices for joint resources. However, this approach requires that the physical proportion of the resource used by products are known in multiproduct settings and the relative periodic demand is known in multiperiod situations. Thus, this approach is not easily used for public goods where the physical quantities used by any one organisational unit does not matter unless a resource constraint is encountered because the amount of public good provided is too small to service all users. The classical case is that of an existing bridge. No charge for use is levied where demand is below capacity but price is used as a rationing device where demand exceeds capacity (Littlechild, 1970 (a), gives a more complex example).

The problem this part focuses upon is that of financing resources with public characteristics in the firm. This problem arises because such resources will have a zero or relatively small cost variable with use associated with a large fixed element. This fixed component comprises items such as, set up costs for the provision of the resource or service and the costs of providing capacity. The problem that arises is that the provision of such resources and services will be at a loss to the providing unit unless some economically sensible way can be found of 'charging' users. The same problem is encountered if it is desired that the market supplies such goods. Goods of this type will only be provided if the supplying firm is allowed to use any monopoly power sufficiently to, at least, cover the large fixed element of its costs and if non-purchasers can be excluded (in contrast to the above definition of a pure public good). Baumol *et al*, ((1988) pp. 301–302) had the insight that this type of cost structure applies to any good that has a high fixed cost component and the provision of such goods will be plagued by the problems discussed here. This provides one reason why accountants have some difficulty in handling fixed costs in any meaningful economic way. Many goods provided by the market have this type of cost structure but can be supplied by the market because exclusion is possible. The ability to exclude therefore allows firms which wish to supply such goods to do so if they can charge a price that, at least, covers fixed costs and promises a normal return (such a pricing policy is called second best because it requires a departure from optimal economic decision rules (Baumol and Ordover, 1977)).

Costing Excludable Public Resources

That excludable public goods can be supplied by the market suggests that public resources in the firm may be of two types: those from which each organisational units can be excluded from enjoying the resources or services offered and those from which at least some units cannot be excluded. Excludable resources are discussed in this section and non-excludable inputs are considered in the following section.

In principle, an economically sensible price can be charged where exclusion is possible. As suggested earlier, firms may have a larger number of tools to enforce exclusion than the market. Thus, accountants should seek to distinguish between those public resources which are excludable and those which are not. The former should be more amenable to charging for use than the latter. However, there are still many problems here. Negotiations between the supplying and user organisational units involve small numbers of participants. Any transfer price that emerges from such negotiations is therefore not equivalent to a market price generated by the matching of demand and supply in the market in a way that is neutral concerning the characteristics of the participants except their demand and supply prices. Intra-organisational bargaining may give less weight to economic characteristics and may rather reflect many other characteristics, such as the organisational status and power of the negotiators. Recourse to arbitrary overhead allocations may reflect a desire to avoid the difficulties that may attend such negotiations. Charging what organisational units say they would be willing to pay encounters the difficulties that these units may understate their willingness to pay especially where the provision will be made anyway and the units cannot opt out of the agreed supply as is often the case in practice. There are ways of obtaining the true statements of preferences but they are quite complex and may involve paying subsidies and levying taxes (see Mueller, 1989, pp. 124–134). This problem may take on a different form within the firm as only small numbers would be involved in any negotiation process and whatever is agreed, each organisational unit will have to bear a substantial contribution to the cost of the ultimately agreed provision. It may therefore be in the best interests of units to accept that they have to make a continuing contribution over time and bargain to achieve the optimal solution from their point of view (see Musgrave and Musgrave, 1980, pp. 81–82). They may also seek to form coalitions with other units. Neither of these processes guarantee an efficient outcome.

The problem of obtaining the true revelation of preferences may be less severe in the firm than for a government. The centre of the firm has a very large number of ongoing relationships with subordinate organisational units and the information systems associated with these give the centre a large amount of information about other units which can be used in seeking to validate and check willingness to pay statements. Especially useful for this purpose will be information from comparable organisational units. The budgeting process and capital allocation processes will provide some information concerning willingness to pay. However if the centre has full access to information, it should in terms of economic efficiency make decisions at the centre and just instruct subordinate units as to their optimal activity given these decisions. In this case, charging for centrally provided resources and services would serve no obvious economic or motivational purposes. Such an approach would be inimical to the decentralised organisation structures widely observed in practice.

Charging internally cost based prices ignores demands for the resource or service and also allows the provider to make monopoly profits from user organisational units (because any charges would involve charging more than marginal cost in order to recoup fixed costs).

The Use of Market Prices

The best approach to charging may be to use market prices where the resource or service can be alternatively obtained on the market. Commodities and services which have public good characteristics within the firm may not have such characteristics in the market because of different technology and charging structures and the ability to exclude. Market prices for this type of resource or service incorporate the exercise of monopoly power at least sufficient to cover the supplier's fixed costs, assuming that suppliers use a public good type technology. If this is the case, the supplier will have, at least, a degree of market power, though the market supplier may have access to a different technology that does not involve a high level of fixed costs. Market prices also may not reflect the same economies of scale and scope experienced by the firm setting internal prices. Market prices may therefore not capture the benefits of 'internalising' the services and overstate the costs of own production. Thus, external market prices may represent the maximum that can be charged and optimal internal prices should reflect the cost structure of the firm seeking to set internal prices. The setting of such internal prices encounters the problem of jointness where the firm experiences economies of scope. Using such prices to charge for public resources and services provided by the firm will only have full managerial and motivational bite if the internal provider is free to exclude internal users, can cater for external consumers and symmetrically, if internal users are free to use the market for their needs and are able to exclude other organisational units—otherwise problems of the free riders type reappear. Even here, the private calculations of individual organisational units may ignore the effects of their conduct on the rest of the organisation, that is the external effects flowing from their decisions to other units. Thus a purchasing unit may compare only the internal and external prices quoted to it in making its supply decision, even though its decision to use external suppliers in some way affects the cost borne by other divisions. This implies that the internal and external suppliers are either using different technologies, operating at different standards of efficiency or that the internal supplier faces inhibitions on its ability to sell freely on the market.

It can be shown that such problems can cause arrangements which are optimal for the firm not to be sustainable where organisational units are free to use the market. By adopting an example suggested by Faulhaber (1975) which shows that provision by a monopolist of a public good to the market may not be sustainable against entry by other suppliers. Consider 3 organisational units which could use a public resource provided by the firm at a total cost £900 which they have been asked to bear equally (£300 each). Assume that each unit could obtain its required supply from the market at a cost of £350 and that two units could be supplied by the market at a cost of £550. From the point of view of each unit, individual supply is more costly than of forming a partnership (£350 + £350 > £550). Thus, no unit would be willing to pay more than £275 as its share of the cost of the resource (£550/2) if provided by the firm even though it is impossible for all 3 units to obtain supplies at this cost using the market. The units would not opt voluntarily for firm provision because they would be unable to agree a sharing arrangement for the cost of £900 even though this is no more costly than buying the service on the market (£550 + £350 =£900).

This suggests that it is not sufficient to require that the charge (however defined) for a firm's provision of a public good or service to an organisational unit must be no more than the cost of the unit obtaining its needs on the market either individually or in combination with other units in the firm. For a good review of this theory see Sharkey (1982) and Braeutigam (1989). Two possible tests have been focused upon in the literature on the public provision of public goods. Here these tests will firstly be introduced as used in considering the provision of public goods to the economy. Secondly, the light they cast on charges the firm could make for the provision of public resources within the firm will be considered.

The two tests to be considered are the incremental cost test and the stand alone test in a setting where the firm is supplying to the market (Fuelhaber 1975). The incremental cost test says the firm should supply the market if the revenues from a set of products, S, smaller than the firm's total set of products, N, contributes sufficient to the firm's revenue to cover the incremental cost of providing that set of products (S) rather than not producing them, holding constant the costs of all the other products. The set of products S is being subsidized if revenues do not satisfy this criterion. The stand alone test approaches the problem from the alternative perspective. It says that in order for the product set S not to be subsidising others of the firm's products the revenue obtained from product set S must not exceed the cost of producing these products on a stand alone basis where production on a stand alone basis would be in a plant dedicated to these products. One important finding is that the application of either test to just the set of products in mind is not sufficient to ensure the non-existence of an incorrectly priced products in the sense that such a product does not just cover its costs. Whichever test is used, non-subsidisation can be assured only by testing all possible subsets of products including the full set of products.

The equivalent test within the firm to the stand alone test would be to ensure that the charges to an organisational unit for a public resource provided within the firm is no greater than the price it would have to pay in the market either buying individually or in any possible combination of organisational units. This test should be satisfied for services rendered by the firm for all possible coalitions of organisational units. The internal variant in the firm of the incremental test is that the revenue received from servicing a unit in addition to the other units already serviced is equal to or greater than the incremental cost of providing this additional service and that this test is satisfied for all possible combinations of units. These tests seek to ensure that prices are fair. Moreover, they do not necessarily optimise for the firm nor can they be used in decision making concerning the optimal allocation between units. This is because these tests assume that the optimal amount of service has already been decided upon. They merely ensure that when tests are satisfied, provision by the enterprise will make units as least as well off as they would be under market provision. These tests are important because if they are passed, charges would be seen as fair and organisational units would not use the market. Results from such tests may also suggest the need for new decisions. The earlier numerical example indicates that such fair prices may not exist. Here the firm may insist that the units use the firm's provision.

Taxes on Public Resources

In principle, the ideal economic approach used to ensure that public goods can be funded is to levy a tax on each user reflecting the benefits they perceive from the public good, assuming that such preferences are known to those setting the taxes. This approach is in many ways similar to that used by a full price discriminating monopolist selling conventional goods who is able to tailor the prices of conventional goods to the individual demand of each user thereby extracting the maximum amount each individual will pay for all units of the conventional good desired. Decisions about the provision of public resources in the firm are however different to those required for a private resource. The firm should extend the provision of a private resource to organisational units until the point is reached that the marginal cost of the input is equal to the marginal revenue to be obtained by the firm from the product of that input. With public resources and assuming the perfect revelation of preferences to the centre, the provision of a public resource by the firm should be extended until the total incremental benefits to all users for which users would be willing to pay assuming that all units use fully the amount of the public resource decided upon is equal to the marginal cost of obtaining that level of provision. These benefits will reflect how provision of the resource will affect the revenues obtained from the final outputs produced by users. Levying a charge or tax to each individual unit equal to the benefits obtained from that level of provision would thus just cover costs, if everything goes according to plan. With public goods more generally, such charges or taxes levied on the users of a public good are called Lindahl prices which reflect the value the individual places on the public good (see Atkinson and Stiglitz, 1980, pp. 482–490 and pp. 509–512 and Cohen and Loeb, 1982).

Lindahl Prices

A major contribution of Cohen and Loeb (1982) was to see that this analysis could provide insights into the treatment of public resources within the firm. They also show how the benefits to profit maximising organisational units from the supply of a public resource can be quantified. The incremental benefits obtained by a unit for any level of provision of the public resource is the change in its profit with respect to an alteration in the provision of the public good—that is they are measure the marginal profitability of provision. This implies that the although the resource provision cannot be traced to any particular use, its impact on the profits of organisational units can be assessed, otherwise the problem becomes one of dealing with ambiguous and immeasurable outputs. Thus, the proportion of the cost of the provision borne by one organisational unit should be equal to its marginal profitability relative to the sum of the marginal profitability of all units in the firm at the optimal level of the resource.

74

One problem with using Lindahl prices or taxes in the firm is that in economics obtaining a specific optimal solution using these prices may require the use of lump taxes and transfers between users in a setting where the users of the public good otherwise may trade freely in the market if they do not like the original allocation of goods. In firms, this may not be possible and dissatisfied organisational units may therefore seek to withdraw from any coalition of units producing a public good for all units and therefore destroy the existing arrangements (see Roberts, 1974). Thus there may be difficulties in using Lindahl Prices to recover the fixed costs of public good.

Cohen and Loeb (1982) suggest that the information required to set such prices may also inhibit their use within the firm. The information required from each unit is the marginal profit associated with each possible level of the public resource. This requirement may run into possible revelation of preferences problems, though, as suggested earlier, these may be minimised where only a relatively small number of organisational units is involved. Where the required large quantity of information is provided truthfully, it may be wondered whether this may be inimical to decentralised management. There is another method of taxing or charging for public goods which is less likely to run into these two problems.

Ramsey Prices

This involves taxing organisational units using what are called Ramsey prices. The usual economic application of these prices is to public utilities with regulated prices which are required to break even. Charging these prices allow the meeting of a monetary constraint by an enterprise required to break even by allowing deviations in pricing from the marginal costs of products in order to cover the constraint. The constraint in this case would be the cost of providing the public goods. From an economic perspective, any deviation from marginal cost pricing will mean that the allocation of resources in the economy will not be fully optimal. Ramsey prices minimise any such deviations and ensure meeting the constraint. Although, it is preferably that taxes to cover fixed costs do not enter into decision making, taxing on the basis of these prices is one possible way of minimising any distortion by basing decision making on Ramsey prices.

Basically, with Ramsey prices, the recommendation is that there should be a mark up on the marginal costs of products. This mark up is not based in any sense on usage. Rather, it is based on 'what the product will bear' where the ability to 'bear' is defined in a specific way. This ability to bear additional costs is measured by the relative constancy of quantity demanded of the product of an organisational unit by the market in the face of a price increase. Commodities showing a lower response of quantity to price changes (having an inelastic demand) can bear more of the cost of the public good or public resources. Such charges have less effect on the total revenues of relatively price insensitive (price inelastic) products. Ramsey prices, thus, allocate markups to products on the basis of their price elasticity of demand which measures the relative responsiveness of quantity to price changes. Those products the demands for which are less sensitive to price changes (those with less elastic demands) bear a higher markup. Those products with more sensitive (elastic) demands are charged a lower markup. Thus these prices minimise the distortion imposed on decision making in order to meet the constraint represented by the need to cover fixed costs.

The best known formula for deriving Ramsey prices is that where products have independent demands. Here the markup equals

$$\text{Markup} = (P_i - MC_i / P_i)\eta_{ii} = -K$$

where P_i is the price of product i and MC_i its marginal cost, η_{ii} the (own) price elasticity of product i and K reflects the opportunity cost of relieving the constraint that fixed cost must be fully covered. This equality requires that the markups in all markets are adjusted uniformly to the point where the firm breaks even (Thus, it is assumed that the firm is unable to further use any monopoly power to earn excess profits.) The element in brackets on the left hand side indicates the amount by which price deviates from marginal cost. The entire left hand side of the equation represents what is called the 'Ramsey number' which is the product of the deviation from marginal cost times the product's elasticity of demand and is constant for all products. The deviation for each product will be positive providing the constraint to cover fixed cost is binding as it will be in the case considered. For the non-regulated firm, the tax on each product has no role in pricing. Such taxes are levied only after prices are determined and measure the contribution required from the product to cover joint and non-separable common costs. Ideally, such taxes should not be used in future decision making. They provide a guideline as to the amount of revenue after meeting variable cost each product of each profit centre has to generate for the enterprise to be sustainable in the long run.

It is not being suggested that private sector firms necessarily should actually adopt Ramsey pricing, though Baumol et al (1988), pp. 191–223 provide very strong arguments that this policy will be followed by profit maximising firms that trade in what are called contestable markets if their products satisfy certain fairly rigorous cost and demand conditions. Contestable markets will be discussed briefly here. Very approximately, these markets are those in which all incumbents and potential entrants have access to the same technology which manifests economies of scale over the product portfolio and exhibits economies of scope. These markets also assume both entry and exit from an industry are costless and that incumbents do not react immediately to entry. It can be shown that a firm that wishes to sustain its output policy in such a market must charge Ramsey prices for its products. Such prices cover long run average costs and yield a normal profit. Expected profits above this level will provide incentives to firms able to use identical technology to enter the market costlessly and to capture these profits and then exit costlessly prior to incumbent reaction to entry.

With regard to using Ramsey prices in dealing with overheads, it is envisaged that firms would continue existing pricing practices but that a comparison should be made for each product of the net revenue prior to meeting fixed costs and the amount required to be contributed calculated using the appropriate Ramsey prices. A profit maximising firm follow the usual optimality conditions and would set prices by equating marginal cost to marginal revenue yielding profits above normal equal to the difference between price and average variable cost, assumed to be constant, for each product. Assuming the firm's revenues cover total cost, the total net revenue from a product after meeting total average variable costs per product should be greater than the tax assigned to that product to cover fixed overheads using Ramsey prices reasoning because optimising would produce the maximum surplus over average variable cost (see Baumol and Ordover, 1977, p. 12). The net revenue after meeting the charge for overheads based on Ramsey prices would indicate the remaining benefits which flow from the firm's monopoly power. If the product is being subsidised by other products, it will not cover the charge for overheads.

This type of tax is not arbitrary in the sense that it causes the least distortion from profit maximising output and is determined by the market conditions faced by the firm. The contribution that would be obtained under Ramsey prices assumes a different set of decisions about outputs than does profit maximising conduct. Ramsey prices will imply greater output than the profit maximising solution because profit maximising prices yield a greater amount of revenue from consumers by restricting output more severely relative to that implied by marginal cost pricing.

In conditions of contestable markets, all firms in an industry and any potential entrants will use this approach to cost overhead resources (Baumol *et al*, 1988). Thus, in such markets, overhead costing will be approached by all firms in exactly the same way. In such markets, all incumbents and potential entrants will face the same market elasticity of demand and will use or would expect to use the same optimal technology. Under these conditions, new entrants will only enter the industry if they expect to cover variable costs and the cost of entry in terms of the investment required for resources that will give rise to fixed costs. Ramsey prices will just satisfy these conditions. Thus the minimum revenue expected from a product in a period will cover variable costs plus a tax designed to recoup fixed costs based on the Ramsey markup levied depending each product's relative elasticity of demand. Thus potential entrants would expect to charge for fixed costs using Ramsey prices in the way suggested above. Incumbent firms must also use exactly the same charging process, otherwise some products will be priced above their Ramsey prices which will invite entry. Again, allocation based on Ramsey prices is not arbitrary and in this case it reflects the market environment and is completely determined by that market.

Thus, it is suggested that the cost of public resources within the firm should be recouped by charging a tax on products reflecting their relative elasticities of demand. This approach is also recommended for taxing for other fixed costs associated with common non-separable resources for which usage related charges are not possible (for example, those with ambiguous outputs) where it is felt necessary to charge users in some way. This is a seemingly dominant wish according to empirical studies on overhead allocation even though many of the costs involved are sunk costs. That those who set these taxes need to know the elasticity of demand for products would not seem unreasonable, given the types of decision generally made at corporate or group level in practice. The required information would inhibit decentralisation less than the information required to set Lindahl prices (see above). The setters of the tax do not need to know the degree of use of the public resource other than that they need to be sure that some usage of the resource is essential for the production of each product.

However, the charges from this scheme are not based on usage and may therefore be thought to be 'unfair'. Ramsey pricing schemes have also been criticised for requiring a lot of information to implement such schemes including product marginal costs and demand elasticities at all volumes of output. For the charging scheme suggested here all that is envisaged is that the firm has this information for volumes within the normal output ranges of the firm.

The practical reform implied by this is that allocations should be based on what a product can bear in terms of its elasticity of demand relative to other products. This ensures that any distortion away from variable cost is minimised and that if such allocations happen to be used in further decision making, any distortion in decisions will be minimised. Other types of practical allocations do not have this property nor are they derived from an optimal economic model. This suggestion is not so far removed from practice as might be expected. Several studies indicate that many firms do allocate fixed costs, especially divisional and corporate costs, based on sales. See for example, Fremgen and Leao, 1981 where over 25 percent of surveyed firms allocated indirect corporate expenses on the basis of sales (p. 50). More importantly, they say

> 'Few respondents mentioned ability to bear as the criterion that was used to select bases but it appeared to be the dominant factor underlying the actual bases employed' (p. 55).

Again, the usefulness of classification suggested in this chapter depends on empirical evidence bearing on the set of hypotheses underlying this classification. The acceptance of these hypotheses facilitates empirical work.

The full strength of the analysis in this and earlier chapters for understanding accounting and for suggesting accounting reform cannot be fully appreciated until the above resource requirements are linked to the factors causing resource usage to vary. This task is taken up in the final chapter.

CHAPTER 4

An Alternative Accounting Report and Conclusions

The first major section of this final chapter develops an accounting report which seeks to overcome some of the problems arising from attempting to reflect technology in accounting. This report also incorporates some of the reforms suggested earlier in this study. The second section of the chapter briefly summarises some of the conclusions suggested in this study.

An Accounting Report Better Reflecting Technology

The first aim of this section is to link up the various types of resources discussed in earlier chapters with the causes of their variability in ways that respect the underlying technology of the resource types. Then, whilst maintaining this relationship between resources and the causes of their variability, it is sought to relate resource use to appropriate cost objects in a way that does not require allocation. The cost objects are chosen such that use of resources are incremental at this level of the product or organisational hierarchies. Thus, attention is given to necessary aggregation of resources in order to avoid arbitrary allocation. The final step is to cost each type of resource in a way that reflects either the opportunity cost of its usage or the tax necessary to recoup non-separable common costs or joint costs in the way suggested in Chapter 3. The next major section of this chapter suggests a format for a routine accounting report that reports resources costed in a way that respects their technology, reflects their economic values and links costs to their causes of variation. Costs will be reported in a way that links costs to appropriate cost objects at the level in the product or organisational hierarchy where they are incremental. Finally, in the report, costs will be grouped according to the types of decisions that cause costs to alter.

The first step in this task is to link up the various types of resources discussed in earlier chapters with causes of their variability in order to discover how each of these categories could be treated in accounting reports in a way that reflects their underlying technologies and which incorporates some of reforms arising from this study. The second is to construct an accounting report that respects these linkages as far as possible and seeks to treat them in an economically meaningful way. Only a few problems plaguing modern accounting are tackled. The format for the accounting report will assume a manufacturing firm but the suggested format for an accounting statement should apply to service firms, though the emphasis on various cost categories may be different. For example, in the service sector resources variable with activities and with the provision of capacity are likely to be more important than volume related resources. Similarly, it may that decision driven resources have especial importance in the service sector.

Linking Inputs to Their Causes of Variation

The approach adopted here is to seek to link the various types of resources to both the factors which change the usage of these resources (cost drivers) and to appropriate cost objects. The resource categories used will simplified versions of those discussed in Tables 1, 2 and 3. The categories to be used are:

Category I: resources the cost of which are variable with production volume

Category II: inputs the cost of which are variable with process and activity outputs. Both these categories include those common costs which are separable in terms of products or activities and processes

Category III: common resources the costs of which are non-traceable and the output of which may be ambiguous and non-measurable Common resources which are separable will be included in those above categories the characteristics of which they share and

Category IV: joint factors giving rise to joint costs, which where it is possible to transform them into separable costs using economic models (usually in a mathematical programming form) as suggested in Chapter 3 will be included in earlier categories.

The resources in each of these categories may be constrained and may be reported in a way reflecting this but this will not be emphasised in the tables below other than by charging for these resources at their opportunity costs.

The number of and the types of causes of variations in the costs of these classes of resources can be very large and are situation specific. Here just a few causes of variations will be considered. These are listed below.

Category 1a: resources variable with output

Category 1b: inputs variable with batches; for ease of presentation this category will be taken to subsume all other process and activity production related uses of resources.

Both of these categories will be subsumed under the title variable with the production programme to incorporate the earlier concern that many batch level activities may be variable with volume, though ultimately this is an empirical question.

Category 1c: resources variable with the model programme.

Category 2a: factors variable with maintaining potential capacity.

Category 2b: inputs variable with other capacity decisions including services and centrally provided services.

Category 3:   inputs variable with managerial discretion (decision driven inputs) and

Category 4:   resources variable with regulatory requirements.

Similar causes of variation could be listed for service distribution channels and for types of customers. However, in order to simplify the presentation, the analysis will be restricted to production activities. These categorisations allows a table to be produced linking resource cost categories to the causes of cost variations.

Costs will be traced to product units, products, to product groups and to cost centres, profit centres, divisions and to the corporation as a whole. Later, suggestions will be made concerning the cost objects to which costs may be traced.

Table 4 (below) incorporates all these categories. The first column lists all the categories of the causes of resource and cost variations listed above. The remaining four columns list resource types discussed in early parts of this study: variable with output volume, (category 1), variable with activity (category II), common: non-separable (category III) and joint resources (category IV).

The rows present possible causes in cost variation reflecting the usage of resources according to the assumed technology underlying resource use. The body of the table indicates the cost behaviour of the classes of resources. Asterisks indicate the possibility of a relation between resource types and causes of variation in their usage. An absence of asterisks indicates that no relationship is assumed to exist. Double asterisks indicate a hypothesed strong relationship between resources and causes of variation. Such relationships are only illustrative as these cause and effect relations will be situation specific. As might be expected resources variable with product output and with activity output are shown to be strongly affected by changes in the production programme. Causes of resource variation associated with the production programme (variation cause 1) are shown as partitioned between product volume and activity usage reflecting that this partitioning is often used in practice. However strong arguments were given in Chapter 2 for expecting a strong interdependence between volume and activity related decisions.

The time period assumed when drawing up this and other tables assumes that the accounting reports are issued monthly as with most conventional man-

Table 4. *The Relationship Between Resource Types and Causes of Variation in their Usage*

Resources:	Types of resources			
	Cat. I Variable with volume	Cat. II Variable with activity	Cat. III Common (non-separable)	Cat. IV Joint
Type of variation				
1. Variable with the production programme	**	**	*	
1a. Variable with output	**	**		
1b. Variable with batches	*	**	*	
1c. Variable with model programme		**	*	
2a. Variable with manufacturing capacity	*	**	**	*
2b. Variable with other capacity decisions	*	**	*	*
3. Variable with managerial discretion	*	*	**	**
4. Variable with regulatory requirements	*	**	**	**

agement accounting reports. The classifications in the tables and their importance will differ substantially over different time spans. For example, more resources will become variable with product volume as the time span is extended.

The pattern of the asterisks indicate that those resources variable with output and with processes are predominantly affected by demand factors different to those affecting the other types of resources and thus may require an accounting treatment reflecting this. Resources variable with product output and activity output are effected by volume drivers. Resources variable with product volume are substantially affected by other elements in the production programme as are activity costs but not strongly by other causes of variation in resource usage. Product volume based resources may however be affected by changes in decision driven costs and by changes in regulatory requirements. Few common but not separable and joint resources are likely to be affected by output changes at least in the time scale being entertained.

Activity type resources are shown to be affected more strongly than product volume based factors by causes of variation outside the production programme and more strongly by different items in this programme, for example the size of the maintained product programme. The table suggests that the input usage of factors affecting activities and product volume are unlikely to affect many types of resources that manifest jointness (resource categories III and IV). This reflects that part of this study which argued that resources that have this characteristic cannot be traced to product or process outputs. Thus it can be argued that the accounting for items variable with outputs is likely to be easier (but not easy) than for other types of resources that do exhibit jointness. Under the assumptions of this study (and often in practice), variations in the usage of product volume and activity based inputs can be traced to the cause of their variation and thus subject to a number of conditions can be traced to the ultimate cost object causing this variation.

Generally, non-manufacturing capacity, discretionary decisions and requirements imposed by regulators are especially likely to involve resources with non-separable common and joint characteristics, though this is an empirical question. They may therefore require a different accounting treatment to those costs which are sensitive to production or process volume. Capacity decisions seem plagued with the problem of jointness as they are very likely to involve inputs with this characteristic. Changes in manufacturing capacity will generally also be sensitive to this problem but less so than other capacity decisions. This is because here jointness in manufacturing capacity is caused not by the intrinsic character of the resources involved or services provided but by the mismatch of capacity with demand and is unlikely to be a permanent phenomenon. Whereas other capacity decisions which include all other decisions to provide services may involve factors which themselves have an element of jointness (examples are an indivisible asset and computer software) or involve services which are intrinsically joint (an information service that has to be used throughout the firm).

Capacity decisions can only be traced to units of products and to units of processes outputs where there is a clear user or opportunity cost and where jointness is not a problem, that is, where capacity usage satisfies all the conditions specified in Chapter 2 as required before a resource can be treated as separable with process or product outputs. The underlying technology of capacity resources for which a user cost can not be assayed is that they are essential to production and are provided with a forecast capacity in mind. In this case, which is frequently encountered in practice, usage as such has no cost or no cost that can be meaningfully quantified. Any cost charged for a capital resource should thus be seen as an example of those taxes discussed earlier that aim to obtain a planned contribution to fund the resource in accordance with plans made at the time to provide or maintain the capacity. With this view, capacity related charges in accounting reports should be seen as a charge for the provision of capacity. Following the analysis of this study, such a charge should be based upon the price of obtaining the service from the market or on the basis of what the relevant products of the responsible unit can bear. This approach applies equally to settings where capital investment is the main method of capacity provision or where the capacity is provided by having the appropriate labour services available. Many non-manufacturing capacity decisions are likely to be decision driven and should be accounted for as suggested in Chapter 3 where the accounting for these costs is considered.

German management accounting theory which takes the view that manufacturing capacity should be accounted for as a provision of a service comes to similar conclusions. However in practice in Germany the charge for manufacturing capacity is based on accounting depreciation (often based upon replace-ment cost). The important thing to note from this and earlier discussions is the very different technological character of capacity resources to those sensitive to product or process outputs. In the later accounting report, capacity costs will be treated separably and differently from costs variable with product or proc-ess volume. They will be charged as capacity costs to the relevant product or organisational unit and the contribution of this unit to those costs will be calcu-lated. Those resources which are either decision driven or variable with the requirements of regulators may include resources which are variable with product volume and with activity. For example, decision driven uses of re-sources designed to enhance quality might affect the type of components used in production and may therefore affect resources variable with output or with activities. Similarly, safety and health regulations may cause the firm to use resources on activities that otherwise would not be undertaken, inspection, for example. In practice, it is unlikely that volume related and process costs relat-ing to decision driven and regulatory resources will be distinguished from other volume or process based costs on a routine basis. However, it may be important to be able to strip out these costs where decisions about resources of this type are to be made. More generally, discretionary or decision driven in-puts and regulatory resources are likely to be common or joint to all or part of the organisation (for example, the resources required to comply with regula-tions concerning the annual accounting report).

The types of resources and the causes of variations in their use determine the character of both the cost objects to which they can be attributed and the char-acter of the costs to be attributed to these cost objects. Table 5 adopts the basic structure of Table 4 for resources variable with the production programme (for categories I and II) and additionally shows explicitly the costs of those com-mon resources which can be treated as separable which are included in these two categories. These should be reported as an element of variable costs in accounting reports. Joint resources can be treated as separable where the de-mands made by each output are known and the resources are constrained in use. Separable resources of these types are shown in the last column of the table with the heading (a) indexing common resources and (b) signifying joint resources. The table indicates for each relevant pair of resource type and cost variation factor the possibly relevant cost objects (column 2) and the type of cost attributed to these objects. Charges are generally based on market prices, signified by numeral heading (i) in the table except where resources are con-strained in use. Charges will be based on opportunity cost (signified by (ii) in the table) or in practice surrogates for it where resources are constrained. With regard to joint costs, charges may be better seen as a tax to recoup the cost of joint resources. Such charges should not be used in short term decision mak-ing.

Table 5 is presented below. The objective of this and the next table is to assign a cost to the resources which is consistent with the economic decision

Table 5. *Resources Variable with the Production Programme: Cost Objects and Cost Attribution Bases*

Factors causing resource usage		Types of resources and charging bases		
Type	Cost objects	Cat. I: variable with volume	Cat. II: variable with activity	Separable common costs (a) and joint costs treatable as separable (b)
1. Variable with the production programme:	Product units/ product/product group			
1a. Variable with output	Product units	(i) market price or (ii) opp. cost	—	(a)either (i) market price or (ii) opp. cost (b) opp. cost or tax per unit
1b. Variable with batches	Product/ product groups	—	(i) market price or (ii) opp. cost	As above except chargeable to activity outputs
1c. Variable with model programme	model and organisational unit	—	As above except chargeable to programmes not to product or activity units	As above except chargeable to programmes not to product or activity units

model used with these resources whilst maintaining the relationship between resources and the factors causing them to vary. Both tables adopt the basic structure of Table 4 and additionally show the cost objects to which costs can be charged in a way that reflects technology using economically sensible charging bases. Table 6 deals similarly with non-separable common resources and those which exhibit jointness.

Following the earlier analysis, the table suggests that only resources variable with output can be charged to product units. Activity costs are thus shown as charges to product lines or product groups because such batch activities are incremental to batches of a given product and the consequent incremental costs cannot be legitimately assigned to product units without denying the incremental character of resource usage. Similarly, the costs of activities associated with model programmes are charged to the model or to the relevant organisational unit.

The relevant findings of the earlier analysis as presented in Table 5 will now be summarised. The costs of product volume and activity based resources are charged to the production programme as a whole where independence exists between volume and activity levels. Without this independence, volume related resources are charged to product units and activity costs charged to product lines or product groups or to the relevant model programme or organisational unit. The costs of separable common resources and joint costs which can be transformed into variable costs are charged to the cost object causing them to vary in the same way as other resources featured in the table. However the unit cost of joint resources treated as separable cost should be seen as an opportunity cost or a tax.

Table 6 similarly links factor types and the variables causing the use of factors to vary for those resource usages variable with capacity decisions. These resources provide capacity to either to allow production (for example, plant, equipment and buildings) or capacity to provide other services (for example, accounting and legal services and personnel management). As those separable common costs and joint costs that can be treated as varying with output or process volumes including user costs are placed in the relevant categories of Table 5, capacity providing resources here are either non-separable common resources or joint factors. Whilst the costs of these resources represent fixed costs, Chapter 3 indicated ways of attributing economically sensible charges to these factors, at least in some cases. These charges are shown in the table. They represent different ways of levying a tax on usage of these factors. It was suggested in Chapter 3 that such charges should either equal the free standing market price of obtaining the services required (where available) or be a specially calculated tax (which may be based on Ramsey prices (see Chapter 3) designed to minimise any decision distortion arising from levying such a tax. In practice, the levying of a tax is more likely as many divisionalised companies do not allow divisions and subsidiaries to use the market for services which are already provided within the firm.

The costs or taxes shown in the table do not represent arbitrary allocations. They are, however, strictly unnecessary for optimal decision making in the short run. Here, the aim should be to optimise the use of variable resources given the level of capacity factors provided. The taxes indicate the contribution required from products and organizational units if the firm is to cover fixed costs and thereby be sustainable in the long run with the existing level of services. The only exception to the above treatment is where the services concerned constrain corporate profit maximising activity. Here for optimal decisions, the price for usage should be based on opportunity cost which really converts these costs into a cost variable with production output or process output therefore they could be reported as part of earlier categories. Where these services do not represent constraints, the cost of maintaining idle capacity should also be reported as indicated in Chapter 3. These calculations will depend on the methods used to charge for capacity. Opportunity cost based measures will measure the opportunity cost of the excess capacity available in the period encompassing possible later uses within the firm and any possibilities of selling on the market. Where capacity charges are based, in some way, on what the market will bear, such a report could as a practical matter show that part of contribution required to meet the tax accounted for by idle time. All these measures of the cost of idle capacity are probably too complicated to

Table 6. *Resources Variable with Capacity: Cost Objects and Cost Attribution Bases*

Factors causing variation in resource usage		Types of resources and charging bases	
Type	Cost objects	Cat. III Common resources non-separable in product units; separable in products/ product groups / organisational units	Cat. IV Joint resources; may be separable in organisational units
2a. Variable with manufacturing capacity	Product/product groups and organisational units	price on outside market or tax; opportunity cost where constrained otherwise idle capacity cost	price on outside market or tax; opportunity cost where constrained otherwise idle capacity cost
2b. Variable with other capacity decisions	Product/ product groups and organisational units	As above	As above

calculate in practice on a routine base. Idle time measures are only required to indicate the possible need for new decisions and therefore some simple non-financial indicators may serve this purpose adequately.

As shown in the table, services variable with non-manufacturing capacity may be attributable to any level in the product or organisational hierarchies providing that exclusion from these services is possible at this level.

The cost objects and charging bases for two causes of resource variability, management discretion and regulatory requirements (causes 3 and 4 in Table 4), are not shown in a table because these causes of factor variability may span all the resource types presented in the above tables. The charges for these resources would utilise the relevant bases used for these resource types in the other tables. Similarly, the cost objects to which resources used to execute managerial discretionary decisions and to satisfy regulatory requirements can be attributed are those already indicated for the resource types involved. However, the initial cost object for each use of factors to fulfil a discretionary decision should be the decision unit which made the original decision (see Chapter 3). As many of the resources involved in this category are likely to be either common and non-separable or joint, it may be better not to distribute these costs to cost objects. Rather, they should be attributed for decision making and control purposes to the organisational unit that generates the fruits of any decision. As indicated in Chapter 3, the resources and costs of specific discretionary endeavours should be monitored and controlled relative to the consumer benefits expected to be provided decision driven uses of resources.

Tables 5 and 6 (and equivalent tables for decision driven resources and resources flowing from regulatory requirements) relate resources to factors causing their usage to vary and indicate the relevant cost object to which such resource uses should be charged. They also indicate charging bases for each type of resource usage consistent with the decision model that would be used with such resources. These tables can be converted to worksheets dealing with actual resources. To do this the amounts of each resource used or available are quantified, priced as suggested in the table and assigned to cost objects. This yields a cost base data which can be used in a number of ways. Analysis by organisational unit or by products is very easy. The aggregate numbers for each cut of the data base can be reported in a number of ways. The next section considers the format of an accounting report that can be constructed using these ideas classifying costs by resource influencing factors. The format illustrated is just one of a large number of possible reports.

Accounting Reports Reflecting the Technological Characteristics of Resources

As indicated in Tables 5 and 6, the costs for resources can be linked to a wide variety of cost objects in either the product or organisational hierarchies in a very flexible way reflecting the technology and structure of the enterprise. The exact linkage selected will be specific to the firm, to the structure of its product portfolio and its chosen organisational structure. The approach used here is to categorise costs according to the causes of variability and to the character of the resources underlying each type of cost and to report all costs in the same categories together. The aim is to initially attribute costs to the lowest possible relevant component in the organisational or product hierarchy. The basic structure will follow the ordering of the causes of factor variability employed in Tables 5 and 6.

The statement ascends both the product and organisational hierarchy. Thus, the report commences with each product and then accumulates the relevant costs and the contributions derived by deducting these costs from revenue obtained from product groups and model programmes. The costs shown are only meant to be illustrative. For ease of presentation, it is assumed that each product can be identified with a specific cost centre. Similarly, the report shows costs by producing department, by organisational group/division and for the firm as a whole. The objective is to commence with the costs variable with product units and the lowest organisational units and then report costs variable with higher product groupings and organisational units. These two perspectives may be more simply reported by providing two reports, one addressed to products and one focusing upon organisational units. The charging base for each cost is determined by selected the relevant base from the charging bases shown on the right of the statement according to the principles discussed earlier. Where relevant, each major product and organisational category also contains costs which are charged to that category as a whole, where it is not possible or wished to distribute these costs to subsidiary units within the category.

In order to make sense of the contribution of each product or organizational category, it is necessary to deduct from the unit's revenue all the incremental costs of the unit. It is thus suggesting a greater use of contribution analysis than is normal in Anglo-Saxon accounting. Such an approach is recommended in this study where resources are not separable at lower levels in the product or organisational hierarchy. This does mean that the analysis is restricted to market based profit centres or an extensive use is being made of transfer pricing. Where neither of these conditions are satisfied other means of controlling cost centres will have to be used.

The suggested general format for an accounting report is presented below. A report of the type shown on the first page of the statement is required for each product/organisational unit.

Thus there would be one of these statements for each organisational unit. Page two of the statement applies to combinations of units and therefore commences by aggregating the individual unit statements. Thus the contributions obtained from each product/organisational unit are combined at the beginning of page two of the statement.

The cost components shown for each cost category are only illustrative and are not meant to represent an exhaustive list. The categorisation of the cost components shown may differ between different firms and industries.

Page one of the statement shows the contribution by product. With multi-products, there would be one of these statements per product. It does this by showing an ascending set of contributions. The lowest level contribution is equal to revenue net of only the cost of product volume based activities. In control terms, this contribution may be useful for monitoring the performance of the operating manager charged with producing planned volumes at a specific variable cost. The next contribution deducts from this first contribution activity related costs and may be useful for monitoring operating managers and serves to remind managers of the cost of activities. These two contributions together may be useful for short term decision making, such as whether to take an additional special order. These costs are those of processes which are those essential to allow production. More general activities which often are decision driven are reported in the third set of costs shown in the statement. Deducting capacity related costs from the contribution net of costs variable with volume and with production activities yields the contribution generated by the department. This may help in monitoring the departmental manager's performance relative to variables within the department's control. Deducting from this contribution the cost of those decision driven services, especially those relating to the product provided by superior organisational units, yields the contribution obtained from the product.

The various costs are assumed to be charged on the basis of which are the economically sensible bases out of the bases on the right of the statement. Generally, product volume related and activity related costs will according to the early analysis be charged at their market price which measures the oppor-

Suggested Accounting Report
Page One

		Charging bases
Revenue from Output		

Less   Variable with output[a]:
Materials and components
Other variable manufacturing costs:
(includes separable common costs and   Market price/
joint costs treated as separable)   opportunity cost/
Wages[b]   tax
Variable capacity costs

Contribution Net of Direct Cost from the Volume of the Product[c]
Less   Costs Variable with Production
Activities:
Set up costs   Market price/
Switching costs   opportunity cost/
Material supply costs   tax
Scheduling costs

Contribution Net of Variable Cost from the Product Programme
Less   Variable with Manufacturing Capacity:
Fixed Capacity costs; depreciation and interest Idle time (tax or   Opportunity cost/tax
contribution forgone)[d]
Capacity maintenance costs
Non-distributed departmental incremental costs including capacity related activities

Contribution by Department
Less   Variable with Managerial Discretion:
Services relating to manufacturing and products   Market price/tax
Non-distributed product incremental costs

---

[a] Any costs in the statement may include decision driven costs and the costs of fulfilling regulatory requirements. Both these categories may be need to be reported separately for some decisions and for some control purposes. Here, it is being assumed that any costs in these two categories which are variable with production volume or activities are not reported separately.
[b] From an economic perspective, wages for many companies are not variable with production and should be treated as a capacity cost.
[c] Dividing this contribution by volume for each product yields the contribution per product unit over direct costs.
[d] The term depreciation is used for the charges for equipment and plant because of its familiarity.

tunity cost of their use. If these factors are constrained in supply, they will be charged at their opportunity costs in terms of the foregone opportunity to the firm of using the resource for one purpose than another. Taxes equal to opportunity cost are charged for those joint costs which are transformable so that they can be treated as variable with product units or activity outputs. Capacity related costs will generally be taxes, except where either equivalent services are permitted to be obtained on the market or capacity resources are constrained in supply when opportunity cost charges should be used. This logic applies to all other resources shown in the statement except that activity costs

---

Contribution by all Products in Model Programme/by all
Departments in Organisational Group

	Contribution by Product	
Less	Variable with Model Programme:	
	Costs of sustaining product group and model programme	Market price/opportunity cost/tax
	Variable with Managerial Discretion:	
	Services relating to product group/ model programme	Market price/opportunity cost/tax
	Non-distributed incremental costs	
	Contribution by Product Group/Model Programme	
Less	Variable with Managerial Discretion and	
	Variable with Regulatory Requirements:	Market price/
	General administration costs	opportunity cost/
	Information costs	tax
	Non-distributed organisational unit incremental costs	
	Contribution by Division/Organizational Group	
	—	
	Aggregated Contributions from all Divisions/Organizational Groups	
	Less Non-distributed corporate costs	Market price/opportunity cost
	Firm Profit	

---

related to model programmes should be charged for on the basis of the market prices of factors as in a reasonable market these prices can be expected to measure opportunity costs.

Additional financial accounting adjustments, including adjusting costs to historical cost where necessary, would be required to reconcile this statement with the financial accounts.

Page two of the statement also provides a set of ascending contributions. Here, however, they are for aggregated products or organisational units coming under the umbrella of the highest superior organisational unit or product programme being considered. It is assumed that organisational and product hierarchies being reported are organisationally compatible. This means that units of the product organisational hierarchy are nested in the hierarchy of organisational units. Thus products (including services) are produced by distinct cost centres and model programmes are the responsibility of a distinct division.

The first contribution on page two of the statement shows the contribution by model programme or product group. This is obtained by deducting from the contributions of the products in the model programme or product group those costs variable with model programmes and those discretionary costs relating to the set of products. Deducting those costs associated with divisional rather than product related discretionary services provided by superior organisational or organisational units and any regulatory costs yields the divisional contribution. Aggregating the contribution of all such divisions or organisation groups and deducting non- distributed corporate costs yields the firm's profit. This would be subject to a variety of accounting adjustments if it were wished to reconcile this profit figure with that in the financial accounts.

The classifications used in this statement may be thought to be much clearer than those in conventional accounting statements. The suggested statement uses mutually exclusive cost categories and exhaustively assigns costs to one and only one category. These cost classifications reflect the underlying technology of the resources being costed. Similarly, a clear logic runs through the statement in that the various contributions have clear meanings for control and decision making purposes. Reflecting this, the format looks cleaner than many conventional accounting reports. The above report is really an ideal. In practice the logic of contributions may be difficult to trace and some costs may not fit into simple cost classifications.

Discussion of the Suggested Accounting Statement

The arguments in favour of the individual components of this statement are contained in the body of this study and in the comments above. They therefore will not be repeated here. Some of the reforms underlying these components suggested in this study will be reviewed briefly below. One aim of the statement is to ensure that each accounting cost shown is consistent with the technology of the resources underlying this cost. The need for this consistence between accounting and technology of an increasedly dynamic character is a major challenge to accounting. Without this, accounting signals may become increasingly dysfunctional.

A second aim of this statement and of this study is to reduce the number of resources and related costs which are treated as fixed overheads in conventional accounting where they would be allocated to products and cost objects. The statement treats as traceable only those costs which arise from resources and costs which are separable with regard to the cost object in mind and collects together those costs traceable to the same cost object. Thus, all costs variable with production volume are collected together and reported separately from costs variable with those activities which are chargeable to the product. This assumes that such a separation is feasible given the possible interdependence of product volume and activities. It is possible to show separately the categories relating to the production programme in the accounting statement because in after the event reporting all the characteristics of this programme are frozen. For control and for decision making purposes all these categories have to be considered together where programme activities are interdependent.

Budgets have to be flexed for all the variables in the production programme not just volume.

The section of the statement that deals with activities assumes that these are traced to products (not to production units) except those activities which are themselves a function of volume (if these are not included in the first cost category).

As was argued earlier in the study, some activities defined in the conventional way are not traceable to products but may be traceable to other cost objects and thus may be included in other categories in the statement. Examples of such activities are shown in the section entitled variable with manufacturing capacity. Such a format is consistent with Cooper's fourfold characterisation of activities (1990). Activity analysis can also be used with other cost variation categories shown later in the statement. Such activities are not shown explicitly in the statement as activity analysis is viewed as a tool for understanding these categories.

This type of statement is very flexible. Thus, it could be compiled using standard costs and budget figures rather than actual figures. The results obtained from the statements can be transformed to reconcile with actual profits by consolidated adjustments at the end of the statement.

The format of the statement, the categorisation used therein and the focus on contributions may seem somewhat different to conventional management accounting statements. However, there is some evidence that contributions are being resorted to in practice where the traditional approach to overheads seems not to produce useful information, especially in the service sector (see Fitzgerald et al, 1991). The format of the statement and the principles of categorisation used are often utilised in Germany and are said to be especially orientated towards decision making and control (for an illustration see Strange, 1991a; see also Boons et al 1992 and Schoenfeld, 1974, pp. 5–39).

The final section of this report briefly summarises some of the major conclusions of this study.

Reforms and Conclusions

It is intended here to review only some of the major conclusions of the study as each conclusion is developed in some detail in the body of the report.

Chapter 2

1). Technology and factor prices are shown to determine cost structures therefore it is important that accounting should respect the character of the technology of the firm otherwise accounting may generate figures which will distort decision making and control. This becomes especially important in the face of the recent and of future major changes in the production environment which are altering the make-up of costs.

2). The technological conditions required for resource uses and the associated costs to be treated as variable with product volume are shown to be very rigorous and unlikely to apply to many new types of resources. The same conditions for the traceability of costs apply to activity costing.

3). The very different accounting problems associated with private inputs and public goods need to be tackled, as do those associated with decision driven costs as decisions concerning these costs may involve very different factors to other cost categories. It is suggested that as far as possible different types of costs should be reported separately.

4). The importance of recognising the existence of constrained resources was underlined as was the very different accounting required when a resource is constrained relative to when its supply conditions do not impose constraints.

5). Applications of ABC require satisfaction of the conditions for the traceability of costs. These conditions mean that ABC cost functions take the familiar linear form. ABC cannot easily tackle economies of scope and common or joint costs. ABC costs are shown to be incremental costs and distortion in decision making may be introduced if attempts are made to allocate these costs to cost objects below the point in the organizational and product hierarchy where these costs are incremental. Additional problems with ABC were also discussed. These include difficulties of linking activity outputs with revenues and that production volume related costs and the costs of production orientated activities may be interdependent. Recognition of the first problem requires that ABC costs be traced to the events in the product and organizational hierarchies at which they become incremental and attempts to allocate below this should be resisted. Attempts should also be made to link activities to the benefits which they provide to the customer for which the customer is willing to pay. The second problem can be overcome by reporting volume and activity related costs together as a combined class with a title such as production programme costs.

Chapter 3

6). Common and joint resources and costs are closely related and cause many similar problems to accountants. It can be expected that increasing number of resource uses will have elements of jointness, especially due to the impact of new technology, especially information technology.

7). Intermediate outputs manufactured in common should not be automatically treated as overheads because many common costs may satisfy the conditions for the traceability of resources and costs to ultimate cost objects, that is, products or organizational units.

94

8). Resources which provide capacity should be accounted for in a way that reflects these characteristics. The importance of monitoring the costs of constrained capacity and excess capacity was indicated. It was suggested that non-financial indicators may help here.

9). Many of the most difficult problems facing accountants arise from decision driven factors and hard to manage resources, several suggestions for dealing with these input categories are made in the study.
One of these suggestions is that attempts should be made to link both costs categories to the product attributes they provide to consumers and the revenues which are yielded from these attributes. With reference to hard to manage resources, the suggestion is made that resort should be made to non-financial information. It is a general recommendation of this study that the use of non-financial indicators may help to solve many of the most difficult problems facing accountants.

10). A number of options for allocating non-traceable common costs and joint costs are explored in the study recognising that these costs represent some of those costs which cannot be easily dealt with using the conventional models.

Included in these suggestions are the following:

(i)   report such costs at the place in the organizational structure at which they become incremental. This gives a example of a suggestion which is made in many points of the study in order to reduce the practice of using allocations,

(ii)   Base any charges to organizational units on market prices, where available, though these need to be used with care or on the cost of any "stand alone" production arrangements that could be made by organizational units and

(iii) Levy a minimal distorting tax in order to indicate whether the costs of non-separable common resources and joint resources are being recouped in the way expected at planning time; thus capacity should be charged on the basis of a tax on those who have access to it.

Chapter 4

11). The cost categories chosen for accounting reports should reflect the underlying technology of the resources in these cost categories and should use costing bases which reflect the reasons for variability in costs.

12). Accounting reports should collect costs together which have the same behaviourial characteristics.

13). A form of accounting statement which reports contributions for each major part of organizational and product hierarchies is suggested. In order to avoid allocation, costs should be reported at the point in these hierarchies where they become incremental.

Bibliography

Alchian, A., 1959, 'Costs and outputs' in Abramovitz M. *et al* (eds.), *The Allocation of Economic Resources, Essays in Honor of Haley B. F.* (Stanford: Stanford University Press, pp. 23–40).

Atkinson, A.A., 1987, *Intrafirm Cost and Resource Allocation: Theory and Practice* (Society of Management Accountants Of Canada and Canadian Academic Accounting Association, Research Monograph).

Atkinson, A.A. and Scott, W.R., 1982, 'Current cost depreciation: a programming perspective', *Journal of Business Finance and Accounting*, (Spring), pp. 19–42.

Atkinson, A. B. and Stiglitz, J.E., 1980, *Lectures on Public Economics* (Maidenhead: McGraw-Hill).

Baiman, S. and Demski, J.S., 1980, 'Economically optimal performance evaluation and control systems', *Journal of Accounting Research*, Vol. 18, Supplement, pp. 184–220.

Baiman, S. and Noel J., 1985, 'Noncontrollable costs and responsibility accounting', *Journal of Accounting Research*, Vol. 23, No. 2, (Autumn), pp. 486–501.

Balachandran, B.V. and Ramakrishnan, R.T.S., 1981, 'Joint cost allocation: a unified approach', *The Accounting Review*, (January), pp. 85–96.

Banker, R. D. and Hughes, J.S., 1994, 'Product Costing and Pricing' *The Accounting Review*, (July), pp. 479–494.

Baumol, W.J., 1971, 'Optimal depreciation policy: pricing the products of durable assets', *The Bell Journal of Economics and Management Science*, (Autumn), pp. 638–56.

Baumol, W.J., 1982, 'Contestable Markets: An uprising in the theory of industrial structures', *American Economic Review*, (March), pp. 1–15.

Baumol, W.J. and Bradford, D.E., 1970, 'Optimal Departures from Marginal Costs' *American Economic Review*, (June), pp. 265–283.

Baumol, W.J. and Ordover, J.A., 1977, 'On The Optimality of Public—Goods Pricing With Exclusion Devices', *Kyklos*, Fasc. 1, 30, pp. 5–21.

Baumol, W.J., Panzar, J.C. and Willig, R.D., 1988, *Contestable Markets and the Theory of Industry Structure* (San Diego: Harcourt Brace Jovanovich, 1988).

Baxter, W.T., 1938, 'A note on the allocation of on costs between departments', *The Accountant*, (November 5), pp. 633–636; reprinted in Solomons D. (ed.), *Studies in Costing*, (London: Sweet and Maxwell Ltd.), 1952, pp. 267–276.

Baxter, W.T. and Oxenfeldt, A.R., 1961, 'Costing and pricing: The cost accountant versus the economist', *Business Horizons*, Winter, pp. 77–90; Reprinted in Solomons D. (ed.) *Studies in Cost Analysis*, Second Edition, (London: Sweet and Maxwell), 1968, pp. 293–312.

Beckett, J.A., 1951, 'A study of the principles of allocating costs', *The Accounting Review*, (July), pp. 327–333; Reprinted in Anton H.R. and Firmin P.A. (eds.) *Con-*

temporary Issues in Cost Accounting, (Boston: Houghton Mifflin Company), 1966, pp. 31–39.

Biddle, G.C. and Steinberg, R., 1984, 'Allocations of Joint and Common Costs', *Journal of Accounting Literature*, Vol. 3, pp. 1–45.

Biddle, G.C. and Steinberg, R., 1985, 'Common cost allocation in the firm', in Young H.P. (ed.), *Cost Allocation: Methods, Principles, and Applications*, International Institute for Applied System Analysis, pp. 31–54.

Billera, L.J. *et al.*, 1981, 'A unique procedure for allocating common costs from a production process', *Journal of Accounting Research*, Vol. 19, No. 1, pp. 185–196.

Billera, L.J. and Heath, D.C., 1982, 'Allocation of shared costs: a set of axioms yielding a unique procedure', *Mathematics of Operations Research*, Vol. 7, No. 1, pp. 32–39.

Blackorby, C., Primont, D. and Russell, R.R., 1978, *Duality, Separability and Functional Structure: Theory and Applications* (Amsterdam: Elsevier North-Holland).

Boatsman, J.R., Hansen, D.R., and Kimbrell, J.I., 1981, 'A rationale and some evidence supporting an alternative to the simple Shapley value', in Moriarity S. (ed.), *Joint Cost Allocations*, (Centre for Economic and Management Research, University of Oklahoma) pp. 53–77.

Boons, A.A.M., Roberts, H.J.E. and Roozen, F.A., 1992, 'Contrasting Activity—Based Costing With the German/Dutch Cost Pool Method', *Management Accounting Research*, (June), pp. 97–118.

Braeutigam, R.R., 'Optimal Policies for Natural Monopolies', in Schmalensee, R. and Willig, R.D. (eds.), *Handbook of Industrial Organization*, Vol. II (Amsterdam:Elsevier Science Publishers), pp. 1289–1343.

Bromwich, M., 1984, 'The Usefulness of Current Replacement Cost Information Within a General Economic Decision Framework' in Klaassen, J. and Verburg, P. (eds.), *Replacement Costs for Managerial Purposes* (Amsterdam: Elsevier Science Publishing Company), pp. 1–16.

Bromwich, M., 1990, 'The Case For Strategic Management Accounting: The Role of Accounting Information For Strategy in Competitive Markets', *Accounting, Organizations and Society* (Vol. 15, No. 1/2), pp. 27–46.

Bromwich, M., 1992, *Financial Reporting, Information and Capital Markets* (London: Pitman).

Bromwich, M. and Bhimani, A., 1989, *Management Accounting: Evolution not Revolution* (Chartered Institute of Management Accountants).

Bromwich, M. and Bhimani, A., 1994, *Management Accounting: Pathways to Progress* (Chartered Institute of Management Accountants).

Brown, J. and Sibley D.S., 1986, *The Theory of Public Utility Pricing* (Cambridge: Cambridge University Press).

Brummet, R.L., 1957, *Overhead Costing: The Costing of Manufacturing Products*, (Michigan: University of Michigan).

Chambers, R.G., 1988, *Applied Production Analysis: A Dual Approach* (Cambridge: Cambridge University Press).

Child, J. and Loveridge, R., 1990, *Information Technology in European Services: Towards a Microelectronic Future*, (Oxford: ESRC/Basil Blackwell).

Christensen, J. and Demski, J., 1991, 'The Classical Foundation of "Modern" Costing', *Management Accounting Research* (6), pp. 13–32.

Clark, J.M., 1923, *Studies in the Economics of Overhead Costs*, (Chicago: The University of Chicago Press).

Coase, R.H., 1937, 'The nature of the firm', *Economica*, (November), pp. 386–405.

Coase, R.H., 1938, 'Business organization and the accountant', *The Accountant*, (October 1–December 17).

Coase, R.H., 1968, The nature of costs, in Solomons, D. (ed.) *Studies in Cost Analysis* (second edition), (London: Sweet and Maxwell), pp. 118–133.

Cohen, S.I. and Loeb, M., 1982, 'Public Goods, Common Inputs and the Efficiency of Full Cost Allocation', *The Accounting Review,* (April), pp. 336–347.

Cohen, K.J. and Cyert, R.M., 1975, *The Theory of the Firm: Resources Allocation in a Market Economy,* (Englewood Cliffs: Prentice Hall)

Cooper, R., 1990, 'Cost Classification in Unit—Based and Activity—Based Manufacturing Cost Systems', *Journal of Cost Management,* (Fall), pp. 4–14.

Cooper, R. and Kaplan, R.S., 1988, 'How Cost Accounting Distorts Product Costs', *Management Accounting* (US), (April), pp. 20–27.

Cooper, R. and Kaplan, R.S., 1991, 'Profit Priorities from Activity—Based Costing,' *Harvard Business Review,* (May–June), pp. 130–135.

Demski, J., 1981, 'Cost Allocation Games', in Moriarity, S. (ed.), *Joint Cost Allocations* (Centre for Economic and Management Research, University of Oklahoma), pp. 1–7.

Demski, J.S. and Feltham, G.A., 1976, *Cost Determination: A Conceptual Approach,* (Ames: Iowa State University Press).

Devine, C.T., 1949, 'Cost accounting as an instrument for pricing', in Lasser, J.K. (ed.) *Handbook of Cost Accounting Methods* (New York: D. Van Nostrand Company Inc.), pp. 70–75.

Eckel, L.G., 1976, 'Arbitrary and incorrigible allocations', *The Accounting Review,* Vol. 51, No. 4, (October), pp. 746–777.

Edwards, R.S., 1937, 'The rationale of cost accounting,' in Plant A. (ed.), *Some Modern Business Problems,* (London: Longmans), 1937, pp. 277–99; Reprinted in Solomons D. (ed.), *Studies in Costing,* (London. Sweet and Maxwell), 1952, pp. 87–104.

Edwards, R.S., 1937, 'Some notes on the early literature and development of cost accounting in Great Britain', The *Accountant,* August 7, 14, 21, 28, September 4, 11, 1937.

Faulhaber, G.R., 1975, 'Cross Subsidization: Pricing in Public Enterprises', *American Economic Review,* 65, pp. 966–977.

Ferguson, C.E., 1979, *The Neoclassical Theory of Production and Distribution* (Cambridge: Cambridge University Press).

Fitzgerald L., Silvestro, R. and Voss, C., 1991, *Performance Measurement in Service Businesses* (London: CIMA).

Fremgen, J.M. and Liao, S.S., 1981, *The Allocation of Corporate Indirect Costs,* (New York: National Association of Accountants).

Gangolly, J.S., 1981, 'On joint cost allocation: independent cost proportional scheme (ICPS) and its properties', *Journal of Accounting Research,* Vol. 19, No. 2, (Autumn), pp. 299–312.

Gould, J.R., 1962, 'The economist's cost concept and business problems', in Baxter, W.T. and Davidson, S. (eds.), *Studies in Accounting Theory,* (London: Sweet and Maxwell), pp. 218–235.

Gutenberg, E., 1951, *Grundlagen der Betriebswirtschaftlehre,* Auflage, Berlin.

Hartley, R.V., 1971, 'Decision making when joint products are involved'. *The Accounting Review,* (October), pp. 746–55.

Hawkins, C.A., 1969, *Field Price Regulation of Natural Gas* (Tallahasse: Florida State University Press).

Heinen, E., 1983, *Betriebswirtschaftliche Kostenlehre: Kostentheorie und Kostenentschiedungen,* (6ed.) Auflage, Gabler, Wiesbaden.

Hill, T.M., 1956, 'A criticism of "joint cost analysis as an aid to management"', *Accounting Review,* (April), pp. 204–205.

Hirshleifer, J., 1957, 'Economics of the divisionalized firm', *Journal of Business,* (April), pp. 96–108.

Hofstede, G., 1981, 'Management control of public and not-for-profit activities', *Accounting, Organizations and Society,* Vol. 6, No. 3, pp. 193–211.

Horngren, C.T. and Foster, G., 1991, *Cost Accounting: A Managerial Emphasis* (7th Edition), (Englewood Cliffs: Prentice Hall).

Hughes, J.S. and Scheiner, J.H., 1980, 'Efficiency properties of mutually satisfactory cost allocations', *The Accounting Review*, Vol. 55, No. 1, (January), pp. 85–95.

Jablonsky, S.F. and Dirsmith, M.W., 1978, 'The Pattern of PPB Rejection: Something About Organisation Structure, Something About PPB', *Accounting, Organisations and Society*, pp. 215–225.

Jensen, D.L., 1973, 'Hartley's demand—price analysis in a case of joint production: a comment', *The Accounting Review*, (October), pp. 768–70.

Jensen, D.L., 1974, 'The role of cost in pricing joint products: a case of production in fixed proportions', *The Accounting Review*, (July), pp. 465–76.

Jensen, D.L., 1977, 'A class of mutually satisfactory allocation', *The Accounting Review*, (October), pp. 842–856.

Kaplan, R.S. and Thompson, G.L., 1971, 'Overhead allocation via mathematical programming models', *Accounting Review*, (April), pp. 352–364.

Kaplan, R.S. and Atkinson, A.A., 1989, *Advanced Management Accounting*, (Englewood Cliffs: Prentice Hall).

Kohli, V.J.R., 1983, 'Non-joint technologies', *Review of Economic Studies*, 50, pp. 209–219.

Krouse, C.G., 1990, *Theory of Industrial Economics*, (Oxford: Basil Blackwell).

Lancaster, K., 1979, *Variety, Equity and Efficiency*, (New York: Columbia University Press), see also K. Lancaster, 1971, *Consumer Demand: A New Approach* (New York: Macmillan).

Laverty, J. and Demeestere, R., 1990, *Les nouvelles regles du Controle De Gestion Industrielle* (Paris: Bordas).

Lawson, G.H., 1956, 'Joint cost analysis as an aid to management – a rejoinder', *The Accounting Review*, (July), pp. 439–443.

Lawson, G.H., 1957, 'Joint cost analysis as an aid to management – a further note', *The Accounting Review*, (July), pp. 431–433.

Lee, L.W., 1980, 'A theory of just regulation', *American Economic Review*, Vol. 70, No. 5 (December), pp. 848–862.

Lewis, W.A., 1946, 'Fixed costs', *Economica*, (November), pp. 231–58.

Lewis, A., 1949, *Overhead Costs: Some Essays in Economic Analysis* (London: George Allen and Unwin).

Littlechild, S.C., 1970, 'A game—theoretic approach to public utility pricing', *Western Economic Journal*, Vol. 8, No. 2 (June), pp. 162–166.

Littlechild, S.C., 1970, 'Marginal Cost Pricing with Joint Costs', *Economic Journal*, (June), pp. 323–335.

Littlechild, S.C., and Thompson, G., 1977, 'Aircraft landing fees: a game theory approach', *The Bell Journal of Economics and Management Science*, (Spring), pp. 186–206.

Loehman, E.T. and Whinston, A.B., 1971, 'A new theory of pricing and decision making in public investments', *The Bell Journal of Economics and Management Science*, (Autumn), pp. 606–628.

Loehman, E.T. and Whinston, A.B., 1974, 'An axiomatic approach to cost allocation for public investment', *Public Finance Quarterly*, Vol. 2, No. 2, (April), pp. 236–251.

Lorig, A.N., 1955, 'Joint cost analysis as an aid to management', *The Accounting Review*, (October), pp. 634–637.

Lorig, A.N., 1956, 'Joint cost analysis as an aid to management: a reply', *The Accounting Review*, (October), pp. 593–595.

Lorig, A.N., 1958, 'Replying to "a further note" on joint cost analysis', *The Accounting Review*, (January), pp. 35–36.

Louderback, J.G., 1976, 'Another approach to allocating joint costs: a comment', *Accounting Review*, (July), pp. 683–685.

Manes, R.P., and Smith, V.L., 1965, 'Economic joint cost theory and accounting practice', *Accounting Review*, (January), pp. 31–35.

Manes, R.P., Chen, K.C.W. and Greenberg, R., 1985, 'Economies of Scope, and Cost-Volume-Profit Analysis for the Multi-product Firm', *Journal Of Accounting Literature*, Vol. 4, pp. 77–111.

Manes, R.P. and Cheng, C.S., 1988, 'The Marginal Approach to Joint Cost Allocation: Theory and Application', *Studies in Accounting Research,* No. 29 (American Accounting Association).

Moriarity, S., 1975, 'Another approach to allocating joint costs', *The Accounting Review*, (October), pp. 791–795.

Moriarity, S., 1976, 'Another approach to allocating joint costs: a reply', *The Accounting Review*, (July), pp. 686–687.

Mueller, D.C., 1989, *Public Choice II,* (Cambridge: Cambridge University Press).

Musgrave, R.A. and Musgrave, P., 1980, *Public Finance in Theory and Practice,* (New York: McGraw-Hill).

NACA, 1951, 'Assignment of non-manufacturing costs for managerial decisions', *NACA Bulletin*, Vol. XXXII, No. 9, (May), pp. 1135–1173.

National Association of Accountants, 1957, *Costing Joint Products*, Research Series No. 31, New York.

Posner, R.A., 1974, 'Theories of economic regulation', *The Bell Journal of Economics and Management Science*, Vol. 5, (Autumn), pp. 335–358.

Putnam, G.E., 1921, 'Joint costs in the parking industry', *Journal of Political Economy*, Vol. XXIX, pp. 292–303.

Ramadan, S., 1989, 'The Rationale for Cost Allocation; a Study of UK Divisionalised Companies', *Accounting and Business Research,* Vol. 20, No. 77, pp. 31–37.

Ramsey, F.P., 1927, 'A contribution to the theory of taxation', *The Economic Journal*, (March), pp. 47–61.

Roberts, D.J., 1974, 'The Lindahl solution for economies with public goods', *Journal of Public Economics*, 3, pp. 23–42.

Sakurai, M., 1989, 'Target Costing and How to Use it', *Journal of Cost Management,* (Summer 1989).

Samuelson, P., 1954, 'The Pure Theory of Public Expenditure' *Review of Economics and Statistics,* (November), pp. 387–389.

Samuelson, P.A., 1969, 'Pure Theory of Public Expenditure and Taxation', in Margolis, J. and Guitton, H. (eds.), *Public Economics,* (London: Macmillan).

Schoenfeld, H-M.W., 1974, *Cost Terminology and Cost Theory: A Study of its Development and Present State in Central Europe* (Urbana: Center for International Education and Research in Accounting).

Schoenfeld, H-M.W., 1990, 'The Development Of Cost Theory In Germany: A Historical Survey', *Management Accounting Research,* Vol. 1 No. 4, pp. 265–280.

Shaked, A. and Sutton, J., 1986, 'Natural Oligopolies' in Binmore, K. and Dasgupta, P (eds.), *Economic Organisations as Games* (Oxford: Basil Blackwell), pp. 111–113.

Sharkey, W.W., 1982, *The Theory Of Natural Monopoly* (Cambridge: Cambridge University Press).

Sharkey, W.W., 1982, 'Suggestions for a game theoretic approach for public utility pricing and cost allocation', *The Bell Journal of Economics,* Vol. 13, No. 1, pp. 57–68.

Shepherd, W.W., 1984, 'Contestability vs Competition', *American Economic Review,* (September), pp. 572–587.

Shillinglaw, G., 1963, 'The concept of attributable cost', *Journal of Accounting Research,* Vol. 1, No. 1, (Spring), pp. 73–85.

Shubik, M., 1962, 'Incentives, decentralized control, the assignment of joint costs and internal pricing,' *Management Science,* (April), pp. 325–343.

Shubik, M., 1985, 'The cooperative form, the value, and the allocation of joint cost and benefits', in Young, H.P. (ed.), *Cost Allocation: Methods, Principles and Applications,* International Institute for Applied System Analysis, pp. 79–94.

Solomons, D., 1952, 'The historical development of costing,' in Solomons, D. (ed.), *Studies in Cost Analysis,* (London: Sweet and Maxwell Ltd.) 1952, pp. 1–52.

Solomons, D., 1965, *Divisional Performance: Measurement and Control,* (New York: Financial Executives Research Foundation).

Stigler, G.J., 1971, 'The theory of economic regulation', *The Bell Journal of Economics and Management Science,* Vol. 2, (Spring), pp. 3–21.

Strange, N.P.J., 1991a, *Accounting For Decline: Management Accounting in Large Engineering Companies in Germany and Great Britain* (Working Paper, Fontainebleau: INSEAD).

Strange, N.P.J., 1991b, 'Management Accounting and Competitive Advantage: A Comparison of British and German Management Accounting', Paper presented to the Management Accounting Research Group.

Thomas, A.L., 1969, *The Allocation Problem in Financial Accounting Theory,* Studies in Accounting Research, No. 3, Evanston: American Accounting Association).

Thomas, A.L., 1974, The allocation problem: part two, *Studies in Accounting Research,* No. 9, (Sarasota: American Accounting Association).

Thomas, A.L., 1974, 'On joint cost allocations', *Cost and Management,* (September/October), Vol. 43, No. 5, pp. 14–21.

Thomas, A.L., 1980, *A Behaviourial Analysis of Joint-Cost Allocation and Transfer Pricing,* Arthur Anderson and Co. Lecture Series, (Stipes Publishing Company).

Verrecchia, R.E., 1982, 'An analysis of two cost allocation cases', *The Accounting Review,* Vol. 57, No. 3, pp. 579–593.

Viner, J., 1931, 'Cost Curves and Supply Curves', *Zeitschroft fur Nationalokonomie,* pp. 23–46, reprinted in Readings in Price Theory (American Economic Association, 1952).

Weil, R.L., Jr., 1968, 'Allocating joint costs', *The American Economic Review,* (December), pp. 1342–45.

Wells, M.C., 1978, *Accounting for Common Costs,* (Centre for International Education and Research in Accounting, University of Illinois).

Wildavsky, A., 1975, *Budgeting: A Comparative Theory Of The Budgeting Process* (Boston: Little, Brown and Co).

Wright, F.K., 1964, 'Measuring Asset Services: A Linear Programming Approach', *Journal of Accounting Research,* (Autumn), pp. 222–236.

Yoshikawa, T., Innes, J. and Mitchell, F., 1990, 'Cost Tables: A Foundation of Japanese Cost Management', *Journal of Cost Management,* (Fall), pp. 30–36.

Young, H.P., 1985, 'Producer incentives in cost allocation', *Econometrica,* Vol. 53, No. 4, (July), pp. 757–766.

Young, H.P., 1985, (ed.), *Cost allocation: Methods, Principles, Applications,* North-Holland.

Young, S.M. and Selto, F.H., 1991, 'New Manufacturing Practices and Cost Management: A Review of the Literature and Directions For Research', *Journal of Accounting Literature,* (10).

Zimmerman, J.L., 1979, 'The costs and benefits of cost allocations', *The Accounting Review,* (July), pp. 504–521.

ACTA UNIVERSITATIS UPSALIENSIS
Studia Oeconomiae Negotiorum
Editor: Lars Engwall & Jan Johanson

1. Sune Carlson: International Business Research. 1966.
2. Mats Forsgren & Nils Kinch: Företagets anpassning till förändringar i omgivande system. En studie av massa- och pappersindustrin. 1970.
3. John Skår: Produksjon og produktivitet i detaljhandeln. En studie i teori, problem og metode. 1971.
4. Anders Mattsson: Dumping och antidumpingåtgärder. 1972.
5. Anders Mattsson: The Effects of Trade Barriers on the Export Firm. 1972.
6. Erik Hörnell & Jan-Erik Vahlne: The Deciding Factors in the Choice of a Subsidiary Sales Company as the Channel for Exports. 1972.
7. Finn Wiedersheim-Paul: Uncertainty and Economic Distance. Studies in International Business. 1972.
8. Björn Wootz: Studies in Industrial Purchasing with Special Reference to Variations in External Communication. 1975.
9. Håkan Håkansson: Studies in Industrial Purchasing with Special Reference to Determinants of Communication Patterns. 1975.
10. Hans Christer Olson: Studies in Export Promotion: Attempts to Evaluate Export Stimulation Measures for the Swedish Textile and Clothing Industries. 1975.
11. Sune Carlson: How Foreign is Foreign Trade? A Problem in International Business Research. 1975.
12. Lars Engwall & Jan Johanson (eds.): Some Aspects of Control in International Business. 1980.
13. Lars Hallén: International Industrial Purchasing: Channels, Interaction, and Governance Structures. 1982.
14. Hans Jansson: Interfirm Linkages in a Developing Economy. The Case of Swedish Firms in India. 1982.
15. Björn Axelsson: Wikmanshyttans uppgång och fall. En kommentar till angreppssättet i en företagshistorisk studie. 1982.
16. D. Deo Sharma: Swedish Firms and Management Contracts. 1983.
17. Pervez N. Ghauri: Negotiating International Package Deals. Swedish Firms and Developing Countries. 1983.
18. Lars Engwall (ed.): Uppsala Contributions to Business Research. 1984.
19. Jannis Kallinikos: Control and Influence Relationships in Multinational Corporations. The Subsidiary's Viewpoint. Application of the Resource Dependence Perspective for Studying Power Relationships in Multinational Corporations. 1984.
20. Edith Penrose: The Theory of the Growth of the Firm Twenty-Five Years After. 1985.
21. Amjad Hadjikhani: Organization of Manpower Training in International Package Deals. Temporary Organizations for Transfer of Technology. 1985.
22. Lars Engwall: Från vag vision till komplex organisation. En studie av Värmlands Folkblads ekonomiska och organisatoriska utveckling. 1985.
23. Anders Larsson: Structure and Change. Power in the Transnational Enterprise. 1985.
24. Bengt Lorendahl: Regionalutvecklings- och lokaliseringsprocesser. Beslut och handling i kommunal näringspolitik och industriell lokalisering. 1986.
25. Howard Aldrich, Ellen T. Auster, Udo H. Staber & Catherine Zimmer: Population Perspectives on Organizations. 1986.

ACTA UNIVERSITATIS UPSALIENSIS
Studia Oeconomiae Negotiorum
Editors: Lars Engwall & Jan Johanson

26. Peter J. Buckley: The Theory of the Multinational Enterprise. 1987.
27. Malcolm Borg: International Transfers of Managers in Multinational Corporations – Transfer Patterns and Organizational Control. 1988.
28. Carl G. Thunman: Technology Licensing to Distant Markets – Interaction Between Swedish and Indian Firms. 1988.
29. Elving Gunnarsson: Från Hansa till Handelshögskola. Svensk ekonomundervisning fram till 1909. 1988.
30. Eva Wallerstedt: Oskar Sillén – Professor och praktiker. Några drag i företagsekonomiämnets tidiga utveckling vid Handelshögskolan i Stockholm. 1988.
31. Alexandra Waluszewski: Framväxten av en ny mekanisk massateknik – en utvecklingshistoria. 1990.
32. Sune Carlsson: Executive Behaviour. Reprinted with contribution by Henry Mintzberg and Rosemary Stewart. 1991.
33. Harold Demsetz: The Emerging Theory of Firm. 1992.
34. Horst Albach: The Transformation of Fims and Markets. A Network Approach to Economic Transformation Processes in East Germany. 1994.
35. Lars Engwall & Elving Gunnarsson (eds.): Management Studies in an Academic Context. 1994.
36. Jan Johanson and Associates: Internationalization, Relationships and Networks. 1994.
37. Eva Wallerstedt: Finansiärers fusioner. De svenska affärsbankernas rötter 1830–1993. 1995.
38. Mats Forsgren, Ingemund Hägg, Håkan Håkansson, Jan Johanson and Lars-Gunnar Mattsson: Firms in Networks. A New Perspective on Competitive Power. 1995.
39. Peter Smith Ring: Networked Organization. A Resource Based Perspective. 1996.
40. Amjad Hadjikhani: International Business and Political Crisis. Swedish MNCs in a Turbulent Market. 1996.
41. Michael Bromwich: Accounting for Overheads. Critique and Reforms. 1997.

Distributor:
Almqvist & Wiksell International
Stockholm, Sweden

ISSN 0586-884X
ISBN 91-554-3885-0